COMMUNICATIONS:
SENDING
THE
MESSAGE

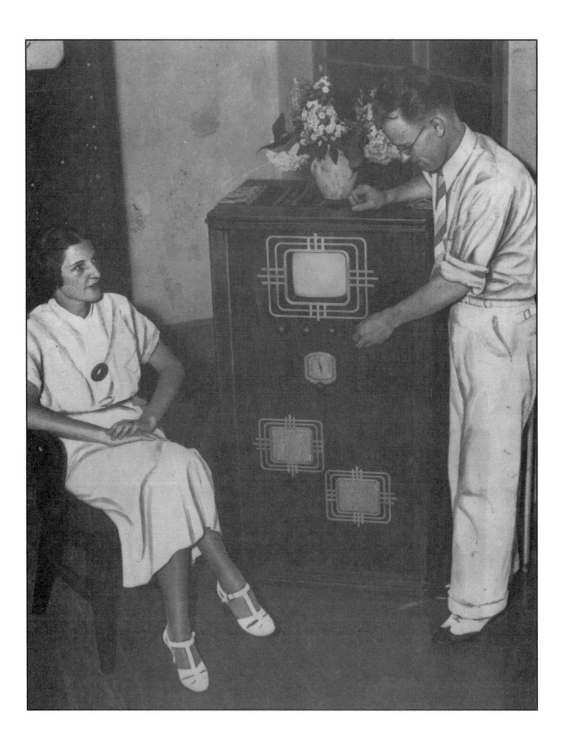

COMMUNICATIONS:
SENDING
THE
MESSAGE

Thomas Streissguth

The Oliver Press, Inc.
Minneapolis

The Oliver Press, Inc.
Charlotte Square
5707 West 36th Street
Minneapolis, MN 55416-2510

**Page 2: Philo Farnsworth, the inventor of television,
demonstrates a combination television and radio to a
potential viewer in 1935.**

The publisher wishes to thank social studies teacher and machinist John Parrish and computer
programmer Jeremy Faden for their careful readings of this manuscript.

Library of Congress Cataloging-in-Publication Data
Streissguth, Thomas, 1958-
Communications: sending the message / Thomas Streissguth.
p.   cm. — (Innovators ; 5)
Includes bibliographical references and index.
        Summary: Discusses the scientists and inventors responsible for the advances in com-
munications technology, including Johann Gutenberg, Samuel Morse, Thomas Edison, and
Philo Farnsworth.
ISBN 1-881508-41-2
1. Communication and technology. 2. Communication—History. 3. Inventors—Biography.
4. Inventors. [1. Communication—History.] I. Title. II. Series.
P96.T42S77   1997
302.2'09—dc21   96-29862
                                                             CIP
                                                                 AC
ISBN 1-881508-41-2
Innovators V
Printed in the United States of America

03 02 01 00 99 98 97   8 7 6 5 4 3 2 1

CONTENTS

Calling from Afar

Imagine that you have to spend a day without using any of the inventions described in this book. If you do, you will be living as people did before these innovations made communication faster and easier.

You won't be calling your friends on the telephone, and you won't be reading any books. There won't be any television tonight, nor any music playing on the radio in your room.

Communications technology provides more than entertainment, of course. Communicating is often a matter of survival. Calling 911 brings the police or an ambulance within minutes. And television and radio broadcast the weather and other information to help avoid more emergencies.

Throughout history, societies have sought better ways to preserve knowledge and to send and receive information over long distances. People needed to know how to treat illnesses, build houses, and perform religious ceremonies. Military leaders had to find out what was happening on the battlefield or with their ships at sea. Merchants and

Long ago, people used to deliver news by using smoke signals, shouting in relays (above), or sending messengers. The modern marathon is named for the hometown of a messenger in ancient Greece who ran almost 26 miles to tell the city of Athens about a military victory over the Persians.

At a time when few people were literate, all documents were hand-copied by scribes, who were highly paid and prestigious professionals.

Johann Gutenberg spent about 20 years perfecting the printing press.

traders profited by learning about foreign markets. Explorers sent home reports of their discoveries.

Until the fifteenth century, most literate societies preserved the knowledge necessary for a stable government and economy by painstakingly copying documents by hand. Because this process was so slow, books were treasures that only the wealthiest individuals and institutions could afford. In the mid-1400s, a skilled German metalsmith named Johann Gutenberg devised a way to create printed books. Suddenly, written information in Europe was no longer reserved for the Catholic Church or the very rich. Printed books now reached a mass audience and a new age of political, religious, and scientific debate soon began in the Western world.

Books helped to educate readers, but people also needed to send information quickly. For much of history, the fastest way to transmit information was by messengers traveling on foot, by horse, or in boats. Faced with bad weather or difficult terrain, they were often delayed for weeks or even months and sometimes didn't reach their destination at all.

Gradually, however, people developed new ways of sending signals over long distances by using visual signs, such as flags or smoke signals, or audible devices, such as drums. Some armies used carrier pigeons to transmit messages. Although these methods were often slow or cumbersome, they proved to be faster and often safer than human travel.

By the end of the 1700s, an ingenious method of semaphore signaling was being used in France. Developed by Claude Chappé, this system consisted

This imaginative illustration shows Claude Chappé (1765-1805) leaning against the arms of his semaphore as he gestures toward future communications inventions—telephone wires and a radio tower.

of a network of high towers built on hilltops. Each tower's tall, two-armed device could be set in various positions to spell out the words of a message. The Chappé semaphore made it possible for people in Paris to communicate with other French cities in a matter of a few hours.

The most important breakthrough in the history of communications was the discovery and study of electricity in the late eighteenth and early nineteenth centuries. Once people learned about how electricity traveled, several innovators realized that electricity, if it were properly harnessed and directed, might provide a way to send and receive information worldwide nearly instantaneously.

In 1775, on the eve of the American Revolution, patriots signaled the coming of British troops from Boston's Old North Church with "one [light] if by land, two if by sea."

In 1800, Italian physicist Alessandro Volta created the battery, a device that produced a steady flow of electric current and thus allowed scientists to experiment with electricity.

Luigi Galvani (1737-1798) believed that electricity came from animals and was their life force. He and Alessandro Volta debated electricity's origin until Volta's battery proved that electricity could be produced without animals by the interactions of metals.

The telegraph was the first device to provide instant long-distance communication. Carrying the audible dots and dashes of Morse code over an electrified wire, it became the basis of even more useful communications tools developed later in the 1800s, including the wireless telegraph (or "wireless") and the telephone. The wireless telegraph allowed ships at sea to communicate with each other and with people on shore. The telephone and the radio further improved long-distance communication by making it possible to transmit the human voice.

As a book preserved written words on paper, the phonograph could record the human voice or music on cylinders of tinfoil or wax. At first dismissed as a toy, the newfangled phonograph of the nineteenth century ultimately became the foundation of the music and electronics industries. In the twentieth century, people developed better phonographs as well as tape recorders and compact-disc players to greatly improve the quality of recorded sound.

During the last 100 years, innovators have built on these discoveries and developed new ways for voices and images to be sent quickly to distant locations. The radio, tape recorder, television, facsimile (fax) machine, and computer are important communications devices that have undergone many changes and improvements. Through the Internet computer network and the fax, businesses can send documents instantly and often more cheaply than by telephone.

By the late twentieth century, as methods of sending and receiving messages have improved, the world has become more closely linked in a vast and efficient communications network. And people around the globe know each other better through the movies, television programs, and music they have in common.

Even though there may seem to be little room for improvement in this network, the science of communications is always changing, and innovations in communications technology remain a potential gold mine. At first, many new communications devices were either ridiculed or ignored. People saw no practical application for the telegraph, the telephone, or the wireless. Later, however, people began to realize the value of more efficient communication. And the stubborn, thick-skinned, and visionary inventors—many of whom had more creative energy than scientific training—finally received the recognition they deserved.

Imagine again a quiet world without paperback mysteries to read at the beach and no way to call your friends from home. You can no longer listen to your favorite bands in your room or watch your Thursday-night television programs. Are you bored yet? You have just imagined a world without the innovators included in this book.

Even after the wireless had been adopted, ships did not always use it. When the *Titanic* sank in 1912, a ship only 10 miles away failed to respond to the crew's calls for help because its wireless was shut off. Only 705 of the 2,227 passengers on the *Titanic* survived.

CHAPTER ONE

Johann Gutenberg and the Printing Press

The first revolution in human communications was the invention of writing. This event dates back many thousands of years to the ancient kingdoms of the Middle East. The written word allowed rulers to publish declarations, merchants to keep track of their trade, and storytellers to record their myths and tales.

Humans first engraved their texts by hand in stone. Later, they wrote on long scrolls of parchment made from animal skin that was stretched and scraped to make a thin writing surface.

The craft of printing did not begin until the eighth century A.D. in Asia. In ancient Japan, Korea, and China, the first printers carved characters into wooden blocks, spread them with ink, and then pressed the blocks down on paper or fabric. In the 1040s, Pi Sheng also experimented with movable type by carving the characters into blocks that could be arranged for printing.

According to the Bible, Moses received the Ten Commandments on stone slabs—the writing tablets of biblical times.

Johann Gutenberg (ca. 1400-1468) holds emblems of his printing craft—a letter punch and a piece of metal that has been stamped with the alphabet.

Clay stamps had been used since ancient times to mark messages with imprinted wax seals, but the Chinese were the first to reproduce documents and books by using interchangeable wooden blocks to press characters onto paper.

Because the Chinese language is written with 2,000 or more characters to represent various words, it was impractical to continue mechanical printing using separate blocks for each character.

Although most Chinese continued to create and copy their literary and scholarly texts by hand or with wooden blocks, thirteenth-century Koreans began to replace woodblock printing with movable type, which by the fifteenth century became the primary form of printing in that country.

Europeans, however, knew nothing about these developments in the Far East. While Chinese and Korean artisans were creating methods for printing books with machines, copyists in Europe continued to reproduce manuscripts by hand. Many of these scribes were monks who lived in isolated communities and spent their days laboring at small desks, writing out religious texts, hymns, and prayers. Using quill pens, they had to copy a text word for word on a piece of stiff parchment. Bookbinders then secured the individual pages of each manuscript between a set of wooden or leather covers.

Making books by hand took a long time—often several months or more. As a result, they were rare and expensive items that only a few people could afford. Even if the Europeans had developed movable type at the same time as the Chinese, the cost of

Even though Marco Polo wrote about the wonders of China in the late 1200s, the Chinese invention of movable type remained unknown in Europe.

When monks copied religious texts, they often added their own thoughts in the margins. Scholars now read these comments as carefully as the original manuscripts.

Because books were so valuable, they were often chained to the shelves of libraries to prevent theft.

In the late 1200s the first European paper mill was established in Italy. The process of making paper had been invented by Ts'ai Lun of China over 1,000 years earlier, in about A.D. 105.

parchment would still have made books unattainable to most people. While kings and popes owned large libraries of books and wealthy landowners had small collections, most Europeans owned no books and could not even read.

In the late thirteenth century, the process of making paper was brought to Europe. Although this process made the materials for books much less expensive, books were still rare in Europe when Johann Gensfleisch was born 100 years later in the German city of Mainz. Very little is known about the life and work of Gensfleisch, the man whose invention made such a significant impact on world history.

The aristocratic Gensfleisches were part owners of the Mainz mint that produced official coins, medals, and jewelry for the city. One of the family mansions was called *Hof zum Gutenberg*, and young Johann began using "Gutenberg" as his last name when he entered school.

Johann's father, Friele Gensfleisch, owned a private collection of expensive books, and young Johann may have spent much of his time browsing through his family's library. While still a boy, he also began working at the mint. Johann may have learned the trade from his uncle, who at one time was the master of the mint. Soon, Johann could cut precious stones, coin money, and create jewelry. In time, he became a skilled metalsmith.

While working at the mint, Johann Gutenberg was struck by a new idea. Perhaps, he thought, books could be created mechanically. Such machine technology would allow multiple copies of a book to be printed at the same time instead of being hand-copied laboriously one by one.

Gutenberg began experimenting with a book-binder's metal punch—a long metal rod with a raised letter at one end—that was used to "punch" single letters into the cover of a book. Gutenberg planned to create sets of letter punches that he could place in a frame. He could then press the frame onto a sheet of parchment to create a printed page. This technique would allow printers to produce hundreds of books in the same time it took a scribe to make just one copy.

Gutenberg made letter punches by melting down lead and pouring it into a mold. But the letters were unusable because they had so many imperfections. They formed uneven rows in the frame. And when pressed against the parchment, the punches left dark blotches of ink in some places and blank spots in others because the surfaces of the letters were not flat.

In 1428, during a revolt by the citizens of Mainz, Gutenberg fled to Strasbourg. There he set up a workshop outside the city walls and spent long days and nights trying to invent a more efficient and precise way to make letter type.

Gutenberg quickly ran out of money because the materials he needed were expensive. In 1436, he took on three partners—Andreas Dritzehn, Hans Riff, and Andreas Helimann—who invested money in three secret processes Gutenberg was developing. One was a new method of polishing precious stones, another was a way to manufacture mirrors—and the third was a printing press.

Gutenberg had developed a way to cast type. Using a metal punch, he made an impression of a letter in a copper or brass bar. He then set the bar, called a matrix, at the bottom of a wooden mold and poured melted metal into the mold. When the metal cooled and hardened, Gutenberg took apart the mold and removed the raised letter. With the mold and the metal matrix, Gutenberg could create many identical letters more reliably than by casting different metal punches.

To produce a document, Gutenberg first cast and set the type. Then he placed the type in a composing stick, which contained all the letters of a word. The composing stick was put in a wooden frame, known as a chase. Finally, the inventor spread ink on the rows of type.

Gutenberg used a press to make an impression of the text on parchment. The press was a large wooden machine that was similar to the presses used to extract oil from olives or juice from grapes. When Gutenberg pressed a sheet of parchment firmly against the type in the chase, the result was a mechanically printed page.

Type refers to the letters that are formed, or **cast**, from metal and used to print text.

This portrait shows Johann Gutenberg using the old form of communication: writing by hand with a quill pen.

THE BREAKTHROUGH

Gutenberg worked several years to devise a new metal alloy for his type. To create many identical versions of the same letter, the alloy had to resist shrinking as it cooled from a hot liquid state. At some point, probably in the mid-1430s, Gutenberg found that a combination of lead, tin, and antimony (a metallic element used to harden other substances) worked best. For the printing ink, he mixed linseed oil and lampblack (a kind of fine soot). This combination provided ink that would adhere to the edges of the type, allowing the letters to print clearly. Gutenberg also replaced parchment with paper. In addition to being cheaper than parchment, paper had a smoother surface and, as a result, reproduced letter type more evenly.

> **alloy:** a mixture of two or more metals

Gutenberg kept his type and his press in the home of one of his partners, Andreas Dritzehn. In December 1438, Dritzehn died. Fearing that his former partner's relatives would claim Dritzehn's investment as their inherited property and make his invention public, Gutenberg ordered two of his assistants to go to Dritzehn's house to destroy the presses and type molds.

Unfortunately, Andreas's brothers, George and Nicholas, had already stolen some of Gutenberg's equipment from the house. Worse, Andreas had not bothered to sign a partnership contract before his death, so the brothers were quick to bring a lawsuit against Gutenberg. The suit claimed a share of the partnership and challenged Gutenberg's right to

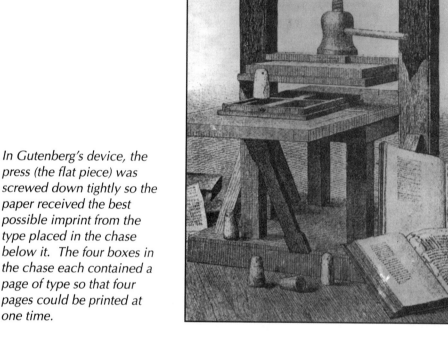

In Gutenberg's device, the press (the flat piece) was screwed down tightly so the paper received the best possible imprint from the type placed in the chase below it. The four boxes in the chase each contained a page of type so that four pages could be printed at one time.

exclusive use of the printing process. In court, Gutenberg managed to avoid giving testimony that would make his printing process public knowledge, but defeating the suit was costly.

During the 1440s, Gutenberg returned to Mainz, which was again at peace, in the hope of gaining support for his project there. Gutenberg was probably the Mainz printer who in the 1450s brought out a classic Latin grammar book by a scholar named Aelius Donatus.

By this time, word of Gutenberg's printing process had spread. Several other European inventors were designing mechanical presses, and Gutenberg found himself in a race against these competitors. In 1450, he asked Johann Fust, a wealthy Mainz businessman, for money to continue his work. Fust agreed to lend Gutenberg 800 guilders (more than $20,000 in today's money), and the inventor put up his presses and printing materials as collateral for the loan. The money allowed Gutenberg to buy paper, parchment (for higher-quality editions), ink, and the metals he needed to print a Bible.

Gutenberg inspects a printed page as a worker waits to turn the screw on the press.

With his assistant, Peter Schoffer, Gutenberg spent months building frames and preparing type for the first printing of the book. Each frame held 42 lines of type in two columns for a single page. Gutenberg wanted the letter type to be perfectly flat and all the type to be absolutely regular so that, for example, each "s" was identical to every other "s." Since certain letters, such as "i," take up much less space than others, such as "m" or "w," he had to adjust the spacing between the letters carefully. In addition to the letter spacing, the rows and columns had to be perfectly straight.

In 1454, Gutenberg and Schoffer finally began printing. Workers operated two or three presses at one time, while compositors prepared the type and laborers hung the printed sheets up to dry. The work progressed slowly because Gutenberg rejected many pages he examined for imperfections.

compositor: a person who sets written material into metal type; a typesetter

Then disaster struck. Although Fust had given him an additional loan of 800 guilders, Gutenberg again ran out of money. Demanding repayment, Fust took Gutenberg to court. Because he was aware that the new process was valuable and that he could make a profit by selling the printed Bibles, Fust may have planned to seize the books as soon as they were printed. The court decided in Fust's favor and allowed Gutenberg to keep only a single set of his metal type. He lost his printing workshop, the rest of his type, and the rights to his 200 printed Bibles.

After taking possession of Gutenberg's work, Fust hired Peter Schoffer (who would soon become his son-in-law) as his partner. Schoffer completed

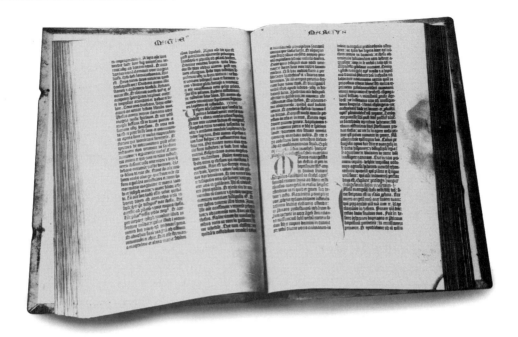

the printing of the two-volume Bibles, which carried no dates or printers' names. With the money earned from the sale, Schoffer founded a printing business under his own name.

Despite the many years he had spent perfecting the printing process, Gutenberg earned nothing from his efforts. There is evidence, however, that Gutenberg again received financial assistance, this time from Mainz citizen Konrad Humery, and that he went into a partnership in Bamberg with a printer named Albrecht Pfister. Gutenberg was probably the printer of a new, 36-line Bible, published in about 1458, that was easier to read than the earlier 42-line edition. Later, Gutenberg printed a Catholicon (a huge dictionary of Latin) and an astronomical calendar.

The surviving copies of the Gutenberg Bible, printed in Latin, are now among the most valuable books in the world.

THE RESULT

Within a few years after the appearance of the 42-line Bible, other printers had established shops in the German cities of Strasbourg and Cologne. In less than a day, they could produce mechanically the same manuscripts that had taken months to copy laboriously by hand.

Printers from Mainz traveled to other German cities and to neighboring Switzerland and northern Italy, carrying the knowledge they had gained from Gutenberg and his assistants. These artisans took with them only the printing molds and matrices they used to cast type. When a printer established a shop in a new city, he had to cast a new set of type.

In Mainz, Fust and Schoffer began printing broadsides—single sheets of paper with type on one side. Predecessors of the modern newspaper, these broadsides carried news, declarations, and proclamations authorized by the city's ruler.

Gutenberg's invention is the single most important development in the history of communications technology. His discovery enabled printers to reproduce thousands of books in the time that scribes once took to transcribe a single manuscript. By making books more widely available, the printing press ushered in an age of wider literacy in Europe. People no longer had to depend on their rulers or the church for information, and a growing class of scholars and writers began to explore revolutionary new ideas in philosophy, language, history, politics, and religion.

Historians of printing can identify the printer of an early book by the type used to print the text.

Printed books sold for about one-tenth the price of hand-copied books.

In an effort to protect his invention from others, Gutenberg had worked for many years in secret. As a result, many historians have given other early craftsmen credit for the invention of printing. People of Gutenberg's time, however, referred to him as the first printer, and eventually most historians and scholars came to recognize him as the true creator of the mechanical printing process.

Despite his legal and financial problems, Gutenberg achieved renown in his birthplace of Mainz. In 1465, the archbishop of Mainz appointed him a nobleman and provided space for the printer to set up a workshop. Gutenberg continued to improve his printing process and train apprentices until his death in 1468.

Printing technology—and the market for books—has changed drastically since Gutenberg's time. In the nineteenth century, machines made printing more efficient by mechanizing all stages of the printing process—from linotype and monotype machines that cast and set type to cylindrical presses that printed on rolls of paper. Now computers are used to set type and create a book's layout and design, and modern printing presses print texts, usually from photographic plates of the manuscript, onto rolls of paper fed into huge machines. Complex automated machines bind the printed sheets into books.

Today, people increasingly depend on sophisticated computer technology for sharing information and retaining knowledge. But the book and other printed texts remain the most commonly used and accessible forms of communication.

CHAPTER TWO

Samuel Morse
and the Telegraph

It was the dawn of the nineteenth century, and everyone was talking about electricity. Alessandro Volta's 1800 invention of the battery to supply an electric current had made possible widespread experimentation with the powers of this mysterious force. The heroes of the day were scientists who demonstrated seemingly magical electrical experiments in crowded halls. Some researchers even believed that electricity was the life force in humans and animals.

From his home in Charlestown, Massachusetts, the young Samuel Finley Breese Morse closely followed the reports of electrical experiments. Born in 1791 into the well-to-do family of a popular clergyman, Morse enjoyed hunting and painting as well as science. His family sent him to two prestigious high schools, Andover and Phillips Academy, and then to Yale College (now Yale University), one of the nation's best colleges. At Yale, Morse studied with Jeremiah Day, a well-known scientist, and took

Scientists had been studying electricity since ancient times, when they found that amber attracted lightweight objects when it was rubbed. William Gilbert studied this phenomenon and in 1600 named it electricity after "elektron," the Greek word for amber.

Samuel Finley Breese Morse (1791-1872) poses with his electric telegraph.

careful notes on the latest innovations in the new field of electricity research.

During his college years, Morse became an expert watercolor artist and painted portraits of his classmates. After his graduation, he sailed to England in 1811 and entered London's Royal Academy of Arts. Morse spent the next four years in England, where he won praise for works he exhibited at the academy's annual shows. In 1815, he decided he was ready to return to the United States to become a portrait artist.

Morse, however, soon realized that painting would not supply a steady income. Although his reputation grew as he traveled around New England painting portraits of wealthy Americans, few could afford to commission portraits—and many clients were more willing to sit for portraits than to pay Morse for his efforts. After marrying Lucretia Walker in 1818, Morse also became unhappy about being away from home for weeks or months at a time in order to complete a painting.

Still, Morse was gaining fame. In 1819, the government hired him to paint an official portrait of President James Monroe. He completed a portrait of the French general Marquis de Lafayette, a hero of the American Revolution, in 1825. When Lucretia died that year, Morse no longer wanted to stay in his Boston home. In 1826, he and several partners founded a group in New York that later became the National Academy of the Arts of Design.

During that time, a new Capitol was being built in Washington, D.C.—a grand structure that

Morse admired. When the government announced it was commissioning four large historical murals for the Capitol's interior rotunda, Morse eagerly entered the competition, confident that the judges would award him the honor.

In 1829, while he awaited the judges' decision, Morse returned to Europe to prepare for the commission he was sure he would win. He traveled through England, France, Italy, and Switzerland to sketch landscapes and cities, and he studied the works of the great European painters at museums.

While in France, Morse saw the semaphore system invented by Claude Chappé in the eighteenth century. The system relied on tall wooden platforms, spaced several miles apart. Operators sent messages from one tower to the next by moving long wooden arms. Each position of the arms indicated a certain letter or number. Using Chappé's relay stations, messages could travel from cities and small towns to Paris, the French capital, in a matter of minutes. Eventually, the system included more than 500 signal platforms. At the time, the semaphore was the fastest method of sending messages from one point to another.

On his return voyage from France in 1832, Morse had the opportunity to think about ways to increase the speed of communication. On board the *Sully*, he met Dr. Charles T. Jackson, who demonstrated the abilities of an electromagnet he had bought in Paris and described electrical experiments he had witnessed in Europe. Jackson also introduced Morse to the theory of English scientist

I wish that in an instant I could communicate information, but three thousand miles are not passed over in an instant and we must wait four long weeks before we can hear from each other.
—a letter from Morse in Europe to his parents

electromagnet: a piece of iron wrapped in insulated wire that becomes magnetic when an electrical current runs through the wire

electric circuit: a closed path followed by an electric current

induction: the generation of electric force in a circuit by varying the electromagnetic field around the circuit

Michael Faraday, who believed electric current produced lines of force. When lines of force from one electric circuit crossed a wire in a second circuit, an electric current was induced at the point of crossing. This meant it was possible for electric current in one circuit to generate an electric current in another.

Faraday's demonstrations inspired Morse to design an electrical telegraph—a machine that could send signals over long stretches of wire almost instantaneously with electricity. Morse spent the rest of his voyage sketching ideas and diagrams for the device.

The son of a blacksmith, Michael Faraday (1791-1867) had only a few years of formal schooling and was an entirely self-taught scientist. Nonetheless, he made some of the most significant discoveries in the history of science, especially in the field of electricity.

In this early Morse telegraph design, a pendulum (center) hanging from a wooden frame held a pencil that marked a roll of paper as the electric circuit was opened and closed.

After arriving back in the United States, Morse began drawing up plans for his electrical telegraph. He designed a wooden frame that would hold an electromagnet, a spool of narrow paper, and a marking pencil that was suspended from a pendulum. As he opened and closed the electrical circuit he had set up, the pendulum swung and the pencil marked the paper strip.

Morse devised a code of short dots and long dashes that were combined in different ways to represent the letters of the alphabet. The sender would make the various letters by opening and closing the electrical circuit for shorter ("dot") or longer ("dash") moments. The receiving telegraph operator would be able to translate the pencil marks quickly into letters, words, and sentences. These dots and dashes would become known as Morse code.

Morse was still working on this invention when the government chose someone else to paint the murals for the Capitol. Frustrated and deeply in debt, Morse gave up painting altogether and turned all of his attention to his invention. Even after he accepted a position as an art professor at the new University of the City of New York (now New York University) in 1835, he put all of his earnings into the electric telegraph. Two years later, Morse was demonstrating a telegraph receiver in his New York City laboratory.

On the other side of the Atlantic, two rivals were competing with Morse to develop the first electric telegraph system. In 1837, British inventors William Cooke and Charles Wheatstone devised the first electric needle telegraph. Their receiver was constructed of wire loops that surrounded five magnetic needles. Signals sent to the receiver allowed the operator to spell out a message by causing the needles to point to letters written on a dial.

In order to be the first to create a workable electric telegraph, Morse needed funding for his project. Luckily, he gained the attention of Alfred Vail, the son of a wealthy owner of a New Jersey iron foundry. Vail joined Morse as a partner in 1837 and brought with him his father's contribution of $2,000 for further experiments. A skilled mechanic, Vail

receiver: a device that is designed to receive an electric signal and translate it into a recognizable form, such as letters on a dial

made several improvements on Morse's original design and manufactured instruments for the telegraph at the factory.

By the next year, the Morse telegraph had gone through several important changes. The transmitter now included a small lever, known as a key. By pressing the key, the operator completed an electric circuit, allowing current to flow through a wire to the receiver. When the current reached the receiver, a magnet in the receiver pulled a small iron bar against a post, which made an audible click instead of the visual mark of Morse's original design. A spring pulled back the bar when the key was lifted. If the key was pressed for a short time, only a short click— a "dot"—was heard. Holding the key down for a slightly longer time produced a "dash."

In 1840, Morse patented his electromagnetic telegraph, but he still needed to publicize his device. Impressed by the invention, the prominent scientists of the Franklin Institute encouraged the U.S. Congress to fund long-distance tests of the telegraph. But the government again disappointed Morse, who had to walk past another artist's murals at the Capitol when he demonstrated his telegraph to members of Congress. The politicians saw the machine as a useless toy.

Undeterred, Morse prepared a much grander demonstration in New York in 1842. He laid two miles of copper wire between Manhattan and Governor's Island and prepared to send a message across New York Harbor. But a boat ran across Morse's wire on the day before the demonstration.

A woodcut of Samuel Morse at about the time he patented the electromagnetic telegraph

patent: to gain the exclusive right to produce and sell an invention for a period of time

The patent model of Morse's electromagnetic telegraph

When the boat's crew cut the wire to get it out of the way, the demonstration had to be canceled.

That same year, another bill to spend $30,000 on an experimental telegraph line between Washington and Baltimore was introduced in Congress. But the vote on the bill was delayed, forcing Morse to wait once again.

Morse nearly gave up hope of ever successfully demonstrating his device. He took on a few painting students and also became an avid photographer, bringing the French art of daguerreotype photography to the U.S. By early 1843, the inventor was nearly ready to give up on the telegraph altogether.

THE BREAKTHROUGH

Finally, on the last day of its spring 1843 session, the U.S. Senate prepared to vote on the telegraph appropriation. Morse sat in the Capitol gallery while the legislators argued. Many members opposed the scheme, and Morse returned to his boarding house convinced that his dreams of telegraphy had been destroyed.

Dejected, the inventor prepared to leave for New York the next day. But during breakfast, Annie Ellsworth, the daughter of the commissioner of patents, came up and congratulated her father's friend.

"What for?" asked Morse.

"On the passage of your bill!" she exclaimed.

At the last minute, Annie told him, the Senate had approved the appropriation. Grateful and relieved, Morse promised Annie that she would have the honor of writing the first telegraph message to be sent over the line.

With $30,000 now available to use as they wished, Morse and his partners hired laborers to lay 40 miles of thin copper wire in underground pipes between Baltimore and Washington, D.C. After the workers had buried 9 miles of line, the inventor found that the wire, which was not properly insulated, would not work underground. He then raised the wire along a series of tall wooden poles and used glass to insulate it from the elements.

On May 24, 1844, Morse finally had telegraph sets ready in Baltimore and in the Supreme Court offices in Washington. Annie Ellsworth handed him her message: "What hath God wrought!"

Morse tapped out the message on his key. In Baltimore, Alfred Vail heard the dots and dashes coming clearly over the wire and returned the message to Morse in Washington. The demonstration was a success!

But Morse and Vail still needed to publicize the invention. Alfred Vail hit upon the idea of transmitting a message from the Democratic National Convention (then taking place in Baltimore) to

In this re-creation of the event, Morse taps out Annie Ellsworth's message on the telegraph as two assistants watch expectantly.

THE MORSE CODE

A • —	J • — — —	S • • •	1 • — — — —
B — • • •	K — • —	T —	2 • • — — —
C — • — •	L • — • •	U • • —	3 • • • — —
D — • •	M — —	V • • • —	4 • • • • —
E •	N — •	W • — —	5 • • • • •
F • • — •	O — — —	X — • • —	6 — • • • •
G — — •	P • — — •	Y — • — —	7 — — • • •
H • • • •	Q — — • —	Z — — • •	8 — — — • •
I • •	R • — •		9 — — — — •
			0 — — — — —

Washington. When James K. Polk received his party's nomination for U.S. president, Vail swiftly tapped out the news on the telegraph.

The success of their demonstration was dramatic. As the press arrived in Washington to report the news of the nomination, the journalists were greeted by crowds—who had already received the news by telegraph—cheering James Polk!

The Democrats then nominated Senator Silas Wright for vice-president. Again, Vail sent the message. Standing beside Morse in Washington, Wright tapped out his refusal to accept the nomination. At first, party officials did not believe Wright was communicating with them over the telegraph. But after sending messages back and forth, Wright convinced party leaders that he really was sending his refusal by wire. Newspapers across the country reported these first news transmissions by telegraph.

Morse code is still used by amateur radio operators.

The term "wire service" is still used by newspapers for the news-gathering organizations that in Morse's time sent their stories by telegraph wire.

After completing his first telegraph, Morse wrote, "I am sure that electricity, harnessed and controlled, will bring more advancement to human sociology than any material force yet known."

The telegraph company founded by Hiram Sibley still sends telegrams, but most of its business is now in other areas of communications.

THE RESULT

After struggling for more than 10 years to realize his dream of electrified telegraphy, Morse finally achieved fame and wealth. When the U.S. government refused to buy the rights to his invention, Morse founded the Magnetic Telegraph Company in 1845. The company built a commercial telegraph line from New York to Philadelphia—the first of a vast network of lines that would link the cities of the eastern United States.

East Coast newspapers began printing news stories that arrived by wire to telegraphs installed in their offices. Commercial telegraph companies carried weather, news, and private messages. Businesses now could instantly communicate with each other; military commanders could transmit orders over vast distances and almost any kind of terrain; and people could bypass the U.S. mail (which took many days to deliver a letter) and send short messages to their friends and relatives in a matter of minutes.

In the following decades, inventors began to develop duplex and quadruplex telegraphs to send multiple messages back and forth simultaneously. Thomas Edison and Alexander Graham Bell were two of the many inventors who got their start by working on new models of the duplex telegraph— none of which were successful.

The Western Union Telegraph Company, founded by Hiram Sibley in 1851, built the first transcontinental telegraph link 10 years later. With the telegraph, the Pony Express—a horse-and-rider

system that had been the fastest means of carrying mail in the West—quickly became obsolete.

In 1867, the first transatlantic wire linked the United States and Europe. The telegraph remained the fastest means of communication for over 30 years—until the invention of the telephone in 1876.

Morse had left his struggles and poverty behind. Now the public revered him as an inventor of genius, and his fellow scientists and the government showered him with awards. On April 2, 1872, Morse died just shy of his 81st birthday, a rich and honored man.

Ships join the first transatlantic telegraph wire. Morse had predicted, "If [the telegraph] will go 10 miles without stopping, I can make it go around the globe."

CHAPTER THREE

Alexander Graham Bell and the Telephone

By the time Alexander Bell was born in Edinburgh, Scotland, on March 3, 1847, there was already a way for people to communicate with each other almost instantly, even when they were miles apart. Samuel Morse's telegraph was connecting major cities in the late 1840s, and people around the world were welcoming the advent of the modern electric age.

Alexander was the second of three sons born to Eliza and Melville Bell. Both his father and grandfather taught speech. From an early age, Alexander was also immersed in the problems of teaching deaf people to speak. To communicate with his mother, who was nearly deaf, Alexander had to stand closely and speak into her ear or use sign language, which he learned as a young boy.

Melville Bell made a good living from teaching and from giving public lectures. In a strong and clear voice, he would read to his audiences from the

Alexander Graham Bell (1847-1922) speaks into the telephone he presented at the 1876 Centennial Exposition.

works of famous authors. Inspired by their father, Alexander and his brothers learned much about the power of words and the capacity of the human voice. In the garden of the family's summer house, the Bell boys would perform speeches for an audience of family members.

Alexander was generally a poor student, but he was a gifted musician and an amateur biologist. Bored by studying anatomy in a textbook, he enjoyed dissecting the dead animals he found in the nearby woods and turned the family home into a small museum of the skeletons and specimens he collected from the wild.

The science of acoustics—the study of sound and how it travels—also fascinated Bell. The scientists of his day had just discovered that sounds are made up of a series of invisible waves that move through the air. When the waves reach the ear, they strike the eardrum, which vibrates against a set of tiny bones inside the ear. The bones in turn send a signal to the brain, which perceives the vibrations as a certain pitch and tone. The greater the frequency of the vibrations, the higher the pitch of the sound.

Although science was rapidly progressing in understanding human hearing, long-distance communication was still limited to written messages, semaphore signals, and the telegraph. No one had found a way to build a machine that would directly transmit sound waves—and human speech—from one point to another.

Alexander Graham Bell (he added "Graham" to his name when he was 11) may have thought

frequency: the number of times a sound wave repeats itself in one second

pitch: the highness or lowness of a sound

about such a machine while still in high school. At the age of 16, he built a talking machine from rubber and strips of tin. He could make the device's tin strips vibrate and produce blurred speech by blowing through a rubber tube. When Alexander placed the talking device inside a plaster cast of a human skull and spoke through the tube, the skull seemed to be talking by itself!

At about the same time, Alexander's father was creating a new speaking system of his own. Called Visible Speech, Melville Bell's system used a set of symbols to represent all the sounds made by the human voice. Bell used the system to instruct his deaf students in the basics of making sounds by moving their tongues, lips, and teeth in specific ways in order to use their voices to communicate audibly.

Many people were skeptical of Visible Speech because they believed deaf people simply could not make the sounds necessary to be understood. To convince the doubters, Melville Bell, with the help of sons Alexander and Melville, staged demonstrations of his system in Edinburgh and London in the summer of 1864. When their father showed them a symbol directing a certain placement of lips, tongue, and teeth, the boys would make the sound. In Bell's system, every possible sound was represented by a particular drawing or symbol. The demonstrations suggested that since speech could be taught by showing how each sound is formed, Visible Speech could serve as a basis for instructing deaf people.

Alexander had already finished high school (at age 16) a year before the lecture tour. In the autumn of 1863, he had gone to work as a teacher of music and speech at a boarding school in Elgin, Scotland. Three years later, he took a teaching position at Somersetshire College in Bath, England. While working as a teacher, he read about an experiment in which electric current was used to vibrate a set of tuning forks, with each fork vibrating at a certain frequency to create a given pitch. Knowing that human speech is simply a combination of certain pitches that produce recognizable sounds, Bell began designing his own sound machine that would use a set of tuning forks to imitate vowel sounds.

In 1870, Melville Bell moved his family to Ontario, Canada. The next year, Alexander left home for Boston, Massachusetts, to become a teacher at the Pemberton Avenue School of the Deaf. Following his father's method, Bell showed deaf students how to speak using Visible Speech.

Bell also spent much of his time inventing. Along with many other innovators of the 1870s, including Thomas Edison, he worked on the multiplex telegraph—a machine that would send and receive more than one signal over an electrified wire at the same time. Bell's design called for a set of tuning forks that would transmit at certain musical pitches, and he hoped his "harmonic telegraph" would be able to send as many messages as there were keys on a piano—88. Although he spent many hours testing and improving the harmonic telegraph, it never worked.

Despite his setbacks, Bell found support for his work from two men he met in Boston. In

Like Bell, Thomas Edison (1847-1931) began his inventing career by trying to improve Samuel Morse's electric telegraph.

exchange for tutoring his deaf son, George, Thomas Sanders allowed Bell to move into his mother's house and set up a workshop in the basement. Gardiner Hubbard, a lawyer and the father of Mabel Hubbard, another deaf student, offered Bell both money and advice. Thomas Sanders and Gardiner Hubbard formed the Bell Patent Association with Bell so they would share in the profit from patents on Bell's harmonic telegraph. In late 1875, Bell's relationship with the Hubbard family deepened when he became engaged to his former student, 18-year-old Mabel.

Bell soon found himself more interested in a device that would transmit speech. He believed the vibrations of tuning forks that approximated speech should also be able to create variations in the electric current going through a telegraph wire. As they received the varying current, tuning forks in the receiver would vibrate, reproducing the sound.

This idea did not interest Sanders and Hubbard, and they refused to support what they thought was an unworkable scheme. Instead, the two men insisted that Bell spend all of his time on the multiplex telegraph. Bell had no choice but to keep working on his telegraph, but he also continued to work on the telephone whenever he could.

Fascinated by new devices, Gardiner Hubbard would invest in Edison's phonograph in the late 1870s.

THE BREAKTHROUGH

The electrical shop of Charles Williams was a center for inventors in the 1870s. Young men, including Bell and Edison, gathered up components for their devices and discussed design problems with the shop's machinists.

By the spring of 1875, Bell had moved to the attic of Charles Williams's electrical repair shop in Boston to continue his experiments on the multiplex telegraph. The financial support of Sanders and Hubbard allowed Bell to hire an assistant, a machinist named Thomas Watson who had worked for Williams. As Bell and Watson set up the transmitting and receiving telegraphs in the attic's two cramped rooms, they could not have known that their work would make them one of the most famous pairs of inventors in history.

Bell had modified his design for the harmonic telegraph by replacing the tuning forks with a set of steel reeds, each of which vibrated at a certain pitch. On June 2, Watson found that one of reeds in the transmitter had become stuck. When he plucked at the reed, a low, steady hum came over Bell's receiving equipment in the other room.

With the current flowing between transmitter and receiver, the plucked reed had varied the strength of the electronic signal, sending an audible sound along the wire. Suddenly, Bell realized that his theories about variable currents were correct: he could use vibrations to send the human voice over long distances.

Searching for a better method of transmitting sound, Bell returned to his study of the human ear. The design of the eardrum—a thin membrane—inspired him to use a thin piece of lambskin as a diaphragm for sensing and transmitting sound waves.

Eager to understand exactly how the ear perceived sound, Bell even asked a Boston physician for a human ear from a cadaver to examine!

Many years later, Thomas Watson posed with the telephone model he and Bell had developed in 1875.

The lambskin diaphragm would cause an electrified wire to vibrate, imitating the action of the eardrum on the bones in the inner ear. For the device to carry audible sound, Bell had to find a way to produce consistently a variable electric current that would change its strength with the pitch of the voice. This problem vexed him for several months.

Bell also had financial concerns in the autumn of 1875. His partners wanted him to work only on the multiplex telegraph and refused to support his telephone research, so he had to lay off Watson. But Bell rehired his assistant after he began to make money by teaching a few classes.

diaphragm: a thin disk that vibrates in response to sound waves to produce electrical signals and also vibrates in response to electrical signals to produce sound waves

That winter, Bell and Watson worked on a new telephone apparatus. A speaking tube on a small wooden base led down to a diaphragm that rested on top of an iron cylinder. The cylinder held an electromagnet that would vary the electric current when activated by the vibrating lambskin diaphragm. Theoretically, this varying current could be converted into audible sound in the telephone's receiver. Night after night, Bell and Watson talked, shouted, and sang over the line—but without much success. Usually, they could make out sounds but not individual words.

Bell was confident enough to apply for a patent for his telephone, however, which he received on March 3, 1876. In his autobiography, Thomas Watson told a dramatic story of what happened only one week after Bell had received his patent. As he was working one day, Watson recalled, he suddenly heard the words "Mr. Watson, come here. I want to see you!" coming over his receiving set. Crying out because he had spilled battery acid on himself, Bell had sent the first telephone message in history!

That summer, Philadelphia was hosting a Centennial Exposition to celebrate the 100th birthday of the United States. Inventors from all over the world arrived to display their wares to the public and a panel of judges. Great crowds gathered to see a piece of the new Statue of Liberty and the modern advances of the machine age. This was the time and the place to announce the invention of the telephone to the world, so the 29-year-old inventor brought his machine down to Philadelphia.

A model of Bell's 1876 telephone receiver (above) and transmitter (below)

For hours, Bell stood by the device at a small table as crowds of people passed him by, taking little notice of what looked like a small, strange, impractical toy. But late on June 25, as the judges came to his booth to look at the telephone, Dom Pedro, the emperor of Brazil, stopped to greet Bell. The two men had recently met at a school for the deaf in Boston.

Offering to show his invention to Dom Pedro, who was presiding over the Centennial Exposition, Bell had him pick up the receiving device. From a distance of several yards, the inventor spoke into his

Almost 10 million people came to the Centennial Exposition in Philadelphia, one of the largest world's fairs celebrating American and international progress.

transmitter the first words of Hamlet's "To be or not to be" speech from the play by Shakespeare. Astonished, Dom Pedro exclaimed, "My God! It speaks!" Suddenly fascinated, the judges now jostled each other to be next in line to listen to the receiver. Bell received the Centennial Prize for his telephone.

Bell soon tested the telephone over longer distances. In Brantford, Ontario, where he had gone to his family's vacation home to rest during the summer of 1876, Bell sent the first telephone message by wire to nearby Mount Pleasant, five miles away. Later that year in Boston, Bell and Watson experimented with the first two-way telephone calls.

In January 1877, Bell received a patent on a box telephone, which had a small opening for speaking and listening. Only then did the Bell Patent Association finally agree that Bell should put all his efforts into his new telephone.

After receiving this patent, Bell and Watson embarked on a speaking tour to publicize the invention. During the tour, the inventor demonstrated his new device by having Watson—who was miles away—greet the astounded audience and then sing (off-key) over the wire. The lectures sold out quickly and were front-page news in the local papers.

In April 1877, the first telephone line in the United States linked Bell's workshop in Boston and the home of Charles Williams in nearby Somerville. One month later, Bell helped to build the first public telephone exchanges, which allowed people with telephones to place calls to each other through a central switching system.

Bell proposed that people say "Hoy! Hoy!" when they answered the telephone.

Newspaper coverage of the Bell lectures had created a growing demand for the devices. That summer, with more than 200 customers using Bell's box telephones—most of them businesses—a switchboard was set up in Boston to relay calls from senders to receivers. At first, the lines were open only during business hours. Doctors and pharmacists had quickly adopted the new technology to improve their services, and pharmacies often allowed townspeople to use their telephones. In order to keep control of his invention, Bell would not sell his telephones. Instead, he and a staff of assistants produced the boxes and rented them to customers.

Bell demonstrated his telephone to packed halls throughout New England.

The early operators of switchboards were young boys. When customers complained about their rudeness, young women were hired to replace them, opening up a new field of employment for women.

The 1886 telephone (above), had only one opening for both speaking and listening. By 1895, a separate earpiece had been added (below).

THE RESULT

Because it was necessary to use wires for telephone service, Bell offered to sell the rights to his invention to Western Union—the largest telegraph company in the United States—for $100,000 (about $1.5 million in today's money). But Western Union thought the excitement over the still-crude instrument would pass, so the company rejected Bell's offer. Soon, Bell would profit from Western Union's refusal.

In July 1877, Gardiner Hubbard, with his partners Thomas Sanders, Thomas Watson, and Bell, organized the Bell Telephone Company to oversee the growth of the new telephone system. As the public became aware of the telephone's potential, many rivals claimed to have invented the telephone before Bell.

Realizing its error, Western Union hired Elisha Gray and Thomas Edison to develop an alternative telephone system. When Bell sued for patent infringement, the company claimed Elisha Gray was the telephone's true inventor. Bell won this case in court and more than 600 other telephone patent cases that he would fight in the next decade.

Meanwhile, the telephone spread to cities throughout the East and the Midwest. By 1888, underground cables began to replace the overhead wires. The first coin-operated telephone was installed in 1889. The late nineteenth century also brought the dial telephone and the automatic switchboard. Signal amplifiers finally made long-distance calls possible in the early twentieth century.

Bell makes the first call from New York to Chicago by long-distance telephone.

After Bell's patent expired in 1893, dozens of other companies began to sell telephones and offer cheaper service through shared party lines. Thousands of people who could not afford to rent telephones with their own private line became telephone users when party lines became available.

Whenever people spoke on their party-line telephones, they had to beware of eavesdropping neighbors.

Bell had a notable career as an aviation experimenter, building aerodynamic kites shaped like tetrahedrons. He also built a hydrofoil boat that raced above the water on a cushion of air.

On June 17, 1914, the last telephone pole of the transcontinental line from New York to San Francisco was strung in this ceremony.

Following the invention of the telephone, Bell's great skill as an inventor led him into many new fields. He built an early version of the tape recorder and worked on improving Edison's phonograph. He also conceived the "photophone," a telephone that would operate by transmitting sounds over light beams instead of electrical current.

For years, Bell presided over the growing popularity of his invention. After financier J. P. Morgan took over Bell Telephone, the company quickly reestablished its prior monopoly. The spread of long-distance service made it possible for people to speak to each other whenever they pleased. When the transcontinental telephone line was completed, Bell and his former assistant, Thomas Watson, made the ceremonial first call on January 25, 1915.

The two old friends were never again to hear each others' voices. Alexander Graham Bell died on August 1, 1922, seven and one-half years after the famous New York-to-San Francisco call. In his honor, all U.S. telephone service stopped for 60 seconds at the time of his burial, 6:25 P.M. on August 4.

Since Bell's death, the telephone has become a fixture in homes and businesses all over the world. At the turn of the twenty-first century, instant voice communication is a simple fact of life for most people. In addition, new telephone systems have replaced the electrified wire. When you speak into a telephone, your voice is now carried over thousands of miles by radio waves and microwaves or by fiber-optic lines—a method of sending signals by light that can be traced back to Bell's own photophone.

The American Telephone and Telegraph (AT&T) Telstar satellites revolutionized international telecommunications when they were launched in the 1960s. The satellites carried devices that received, amplified, and rebroadcast electronic signals. This improved international telephone transmission by avoiding the interference caused by the curvature of the earth.

Phone lines also carry computer transmissions, such as e-mail, Internet data, on-line programs, and video signals. Perhaps not even Alexander Graham Bell could have seen the hidden potential of the little machine that Western Union unwisely refused to buy in 1877.

CHAPTER FOUR

Thomas Edison and the Phonograph

The nineteenth century spawned an era of rapid change and innovation as new technology transformed the nation into an industrial power. Better communications helped fuel economic growth by bringing buyers and sellers closer together—even when they were hundreds or thousands of miles apart. The most important inventions in the field were Samuel Morse's telegraph and Alexander Graham Bell's telephone.

Inventors kept busy designing hundreds of other innovations in communications technology. The first phonograph, the first mimeograph machine, the first microphone, and the first motion picture projector would soon appear, as would the most important invention of the age—the incandescent light bulb. All of these were the work of Thomas Alva Edison.

On February 11, 1847, Thomas Edison was born in the small town of Milan, Ohio. When he

On June 16, 1888, Thomas Edison (1847-1931) listens to an improved version of his phonograph after working for three days straight.

The future inventor at age 14, not long before he began to work as a telegraph operator

was very young, his family moved to Port Huron, Michigan, to seek work for his father, a carpenter and lumber dealer who sometimes had to struggle to support his family. Nicknamed Al, young Edison was a mischievous boy who quickly grew bored with classroom lessons, prompting one teacher to conclude he was dimwitted.

Curious about chemistry, electricity, and other scientific subjects, Al set up a laboratory in the basement of his home. After reading about the recent invention of Samuel Morse, he built his own working telegraph set.

At the age of 12, Al got a job selling newspapers on a train. When he wasn't offering the latest dispatches to the passengers, he worked in a laboratory he had set up in a baggage car. One day, Al spilled flammable chemicals and started the car on fire. The furious conductor kicked the boy off the train at the next station.

In 1862, when he was 15 years old, Al began to learn telegraphing. Train companies were among the major users of Morse's telegraph, employing operators to send reports of arrivals, departures, and other information from one station to the next along the railroad tracks. Al's work would take him throughout the South and the Midwest.

Edison was a careless employee who masked his slow telegraphing by loosely transcribing the messages he received. Absorbed by his experiments, he would lose interest in his work. At one point, he devised a mechanism that would send telegraph signals automatically while he was sleeping or reading or working on a new machine. This device often got him into trouble. Edison would find himself wandering from one telegraph station to the next as more than one exasperated employer fired him.

The inventor's short career as a telegraph operator did give him valuable experience in the practical use of communications devices. Seeking a way to improve the telegraph, he designed and built a telegraph "recorder" that would convert the dots and dashes into short and long perforations on a roll of paper. A slow operator (like Edison) could save the marked paper and play the message back later.

In January 1869, just a few months after joining Western Union in Boston, Edison quit to become a full-time inventor. At this time, the telegraph was still the principal means of long-distance communication. Knowing that great riches were waiting for anyone who could improve its technology, many inventors were working on the device.

Edison and his competitors, including Alexander Graham Bell, were trying improve Morse's telegraph so it could carry a signal in more than one direction at a time. Edison attempted to create a "duplex" telegraph that could carry messages simultaneously in both directions. The duplex would theoretically work twice as efficiently as a one-way telegraph line, and telegraph companies would profit from the increased business. But the duplex machines already in existence often broke down, which made them impractical for commercial use. Unfortunately, Edison's duplexes were no more reliable.

Edison had also been working on other devices and business opportunities. The most promising one was a price ticker that gold speculators could use to transmit prices by wire from the Boston Gold Exchange to their offices. Materials proved costly, however, and Edison and his partners were not very good at managing money. In the spring of 1869, the young inventor left Boston for New York City, where he believed there were better opportunities for selling his inventions.

Edison got his first big break from Franklin Pope, who had praised one of Edison's duplex telegraphs in his journal, *Telegrapher*. Pope worked at the Gold Indicator Company and offered Edison a place to live in the company's basement. One day, when the firm's gold-price ticker system broke down, Edison was able to repair it quickly and avert a catastrophe. This feat prompted company president Samuel Laws to offer him a job.

As soon as Edison began producing machines for the Gold Indicator Company, his ingenious designs caught the attention of other companies. Already a shrewd young man, Edison became aware of the advantages of forming multiple business partnerships and agreements. As a result, over the next few years, he entered into a dizzying array of complex business associations.

After Samuel Laws sold the Gold Indicator Company to the Gold and Stock Company, Edison, Franklin Pope, and another telegraphing engineer named James Ashley formed their own company in October 1869—Pope, Edison and Company.

Pope, Edison and Company leased gold-ticker lines, installed equipment, and built alarms. The company's profitable gold-price service attracted the attention of the Gold and Stock Company, the company that had purchased the Gold Indicator Company only a few months before. In the spring of 1870, Pope, Edison and Company merged with Gold and Stock.

This merger didn't reduce Edison's involvement in other business deals. He produced the Universal Stock Printer to transmit stock prices to clients. The machine proved so useful that Marshall Lefferts, the president of Gold and Stock, offered Edison $30,000 (more than $370,000 in today's money) to supply his company with the printers. This device would become the basis of the modern financial network and make Edison a wealthy man.

Edison met his future wife, Mary Stilwell, when she was working at Gold and Stock.

An Edison Universal Stock Printer from about 1873. Like a telegraph, the printer received electronic signals—information on stock prices—that it printed out on ticker tape.

Since Edison would receive this sum only if the printer was successful, he still needed funding for his other projects. Philadelphia financier George Harrington concluded Edison was a good risk and helped him find a new, larger workshop in Newark, New Jersey, in late 1870. There the inventor tried to produce an automatic telegraph. Another venture, with William Unger, produced printers profitably and helped to fund Edison's ever-increasing list of project ideas. In the midst of all these business associations, Edison continued to work on improving the duplex telegraph for Western Union.

By the mid-1870s, Edison was finally beginning to reap the financial rewards of his feverish work. In 1876, he was able to build a private research laboratory at Menlo Park, New Jersey—a laboratory dedicated to completing work on the inventions that most interested him rather than those his financial backers found most promising. In his office and library, Edison designed hundreds of new devices, many in the field of communications.

One of these was the mimeograph machine, which created multiple copies of a single page. The operator punctured thick wax paper with letters and words to make a master document. The operator then set the master around a metal cylinder. Ink on the cylinder was transferred to blank pages through the holes formed by the letter punch, creating an exact copy of the original document.

With funding from Western Union, Edison also made an important improvement to Alexander Graham Bell's telephone transmitter. The telephone

One investor exclaimed he would believe it if he were told Edison had invented a machine to make babies!

was plagued with static and low-quality sound. Edison found a way to amplify the sound of a voice heard in the telephone receiver. His claim to the rights to telephones using his improved transmitter sent him into a lengthy legal battle with the telephone's inventor, Alexander Graham Bell.

In the summer of 1877, one year after Bell had introduced his box telephone to the public at the Centennial Exposition, Edison began working on a way to record telephone messages for delivery so that it would be possible to send and receive multiple messages. From this idea came the phonograph— Edison's only entirely original invention.

Edison planned to record messages on waxed paper placed on a metal disk. In his early experiments, he noticed a hum when a needle ran over the paper it had just marked. He realized the vibrations of the needle must have created the hum. Using the principle that all sounds are formed by invisible vibrations in the air, Edison devised an experiment. He placed a metal diaphragm over a needle and set the needle on a disk of recording paper. As he shouted through the diaphragm, making it vibrate, he noticed that the needle's point was engraving small marks as he pulled the paper past it. The device was creating a visible record of sound!

If he could make a record of sound, perhaps he also could play it back by pulling the paper through another needle that would cause an attached diaphragm to vibrate as the needle passed over the marks. After many false starts, Edison sketched a device that featured a small cylinder with diaphragms

Alexander Graham Bell (1847-1922) fought hundreds of claims over the rights to his telephone.

at either end. One diaphragm and needle would record the sound, and the other would play it back when an operator turned the cylinder with a hand crank. A small speaking tube channeled the sound waves into the recording diaphragm, which was linked to a needle resting against the cylinder.

Edison planned to wrap a sheet of tinfoil around the cylinder. He believed that when the needle was activated by sound through the diaphragm, it would permanently engrave vibrations in the foil, effectively recording sound. Edison hoped that the sound would be repeated when he placed the marked tinfoil under the needle of the playback diaphragm and cranked the cylinder.

Edison with most of his staff at Menlo Park in 1880. Top row (left to right): James Seymour, John Lawson, John Randolph, George Carman, Frank McLaughlin, and John Ott; middle row (left to right): Alfred Haid, Francis Upton, Edison, and Charles Batchelor; bottom row (left to right): Francis Jehl, Martin Force, Alf Swanson, and Stockton Griffin.

THE BREAKTHROUGH

Edison and his assistants had been designing and building "speaking telegraph" devices with different materials for months with little success. So when Edison sketched an idea on paper and handed it to one of his engineers, a Swiss clockmaker named John Kruesi, Kruesi doubted the machine would work. Betting Edison $2 that the device would fail, Kruesi nevertheless built it. On December 4, 1877, Edison, Kruesi, and several other workers at the Menlo Park shop gathered in front of the machine at a table. As Kruesi turned the cylinder and set the needle against it, Edison shouted the words to a children's poem into the speaking tube:

John Kruesi, a talented engineer, worked with Edison for about 30 years and made the models of all of Edison's inventions in the Newark and Menlo Park workshops.

> Mary had a little lamb,
> Its fleece was white as snow.
> And everywhere that Mary went,
> The lamb was sure to go.

Kruesi set the playback needle at the beginning and began to crank the device. Much to the astonishment of Edison and the men surrounding him, the voice of the inventor came through the speaking tube. The phonograph was born!

In the next few days, Edison went to New York City to demonstrate his tinfoil phonograph to the editor of *Scientific American*. News of the amazing new recording device spread quickly. In the spring of 1878, before a meeting of eminent scientists in Washington, D.C., the phonograph onstage played,

In the 1870s, people who wrote shorthand (a system of rapid handwriting in code) were called phonographers, or "sound writers."

One of Edison's partners in the phonograph company was Gardiner Hubbard, Alexander Graham Bell's father-in-law.

"The speaking phonograph has the honor of presenting itself to the Academy of Sciences." The machine also was demonstrated to the director of the Smithsonian Institution and U.S. President Rutherford B. Hayes. Pleased with the success, Edison formed the Edison Speaking Phonograph Company in April 1878. Soon the inventor made an agreement with Sigmund Bergmann, a former assistant, to manufacture the phonographs.

Edison, however, realized that the tinfoil phonograph was a very crude device that needed several improvements before it could be produced and sold in large numbers. For one thing, the tinfoil cylinder wore out after only a few playbacks. So he

Edison's original tinfoil phonograph from 1877

put the invention aside for a decade while he worked on creating a simple and inexpensive light bulb.

In the meantime, other inventors were also working on the phonograph. By the late 1880s, Edison saw he was in danger of losing control of one of his most important inventions, so he turned

Edison poses with a new version of the tinfoil phonograph in April 1878.

his attention back to it. In 1887, he adopted a wax cylinder that proved more durable than the earlier tinfoil one. (An inventor working in the labs of Alexander Graham Bell had developed the wax version.) Edison also created an automatic cranking device. Turning the cylinder by hand resulted in a variable rate of speed. Since changing speed also changed the frequency and pitch of the sounds recorded in the cylinder, adding a motor to the cranking mechanism was an important advance.

Edison also improved the recording needle by designing new sapphire points for recording and playback. The former recording needle, which was used to make impressions in the cylinder, had a straight cutting edge. Edison's new playback needle was rounded so it would not wear out or damage the grooves of the cylinder.

In 1888, Edison began mass-producing his improved phonograph. With financier Jesse Lippincott—who also owned the rights to two other phonograph inventions—he formed the North American Phonograph Company to record, duplicate, and sell music. Over the course of the next decade, a public eager for entertainment at home bought more than 1 million phonographs.

Edison believed that "phonograms"—self-produced recordings of messages that could be played on the phonograph—would replace written correspondence.

THE RESULT

By the turn of the century, the modern recording industry had found a wide audience. To improve sound quality, Edison designed the first microphone to transmit sound waves electronically to the recording cylinder. The microphone replaced the speaking tube and diaphragms of his earlier models.

In 1900, inventor Emile Berliner made another important improvement to the phonograph. He replaced the cylinder with a flat disk, which recorded sound waves from side to side, instead of up and down in the grooves of the cylinder. Edison did not begin to work on a disk phonograph until 1909.

Edison with his 1906 cylinder phonograph. Berliner's disk phonograph produced a more precise sound because it recorded a wider range of sound frequencies.

This 1894 film of an Edison employee sneezing was the first motion picture submitted for copyright.

Another invention that would impact the twentieth-century recording industry began in an attempt to record telephone conversations. In 1899, Danish engineer Valdemar Poulsen invented the telegraphone, a device that recorded sound vibrations in telephone calls on rapidly unspooling steel wire. The telegraphone was the ancestor of the modern tape recorder.

Thomas Edison's genius for devising practical means for better communication eventually led him into the new field of motion pictures. In 1889, Edison and his assistant William Dickson created the "Kineto-phonograph," or kinetograph, a device that recorded a series of still images in rapid succession. Because each picture in the series showed a slightly different version of the scene, the kinetoscope that played the film gave the viewer an illusion of movement. In the late nineteenth century, kinetoscope parlors allowed customers to watch these short films for a fee of five cents each.

To create short films for the kinetoscope, Edison also built the first movie studio. It consisted of a large room that was placed on a center pivot. An opening in the ceiling allowed natural light into the room for filming, and the pivot allowed Edison to turn the room to follow the position of the sun.

Recorded music and motion pictures became the most popular forms of entertainment at the beginning of the twentieth century. As the United States and other countries grew wealthier, people found themselves with more time and money for leisure activities. Musical recordings and motion pictures captured huge audiences all over the world and spawned thousands of new businesses devoted exclusively to entertainment. These industries relied heavily on the innovations of Edison, who began his career by sending simple electronic signals along railroad telegraph wires. By the time of his death on October 18, 1931, the inventor had been awarded more than 1,000 patents.

Edison so loved the telegraph that he had nicknamed his children "Dot" and "Dash" for the two signals given by the device. Here in the library of his West Orange, New Jersey, laboratory, 73-year-old Edison was still using his telegraph in 1920.

CHAPTER FIVE

Guglielmo Marconi and the Wireless

By the 1880s, Samuel Morse's telegraph had become the most important instrument of international communication. A network of telegraph stations allowed operators to send messages and news articles from city to city within the United States and between North America and Europe. If you had looked up at the sky in any major city of the time, you would have seen a maze of telegraph wires. These wires even stretched 3,000 miles across the floor of the Atlantic Ocean. After the invention of the telephone in 1876, a similar network of wires carried the human voice for miles and miles.

Yet electricity was still a mystery to many people. Most were not sure where it came from or what it could do. Even more mysterious was the idea of traveling parcels of electric energy—electromagnetic waves—which, James Clerk Maxwell theorized in the mid-1800s, moved at the speed of light through invisible electromagnetic fields.

Because of his invention, Guglielmo Marconi (1874-1937) became a celebrity and made friends with such international figures as Pope Pius XI, Queen Victoria of England, and Italian dictator Benito Mussolini.

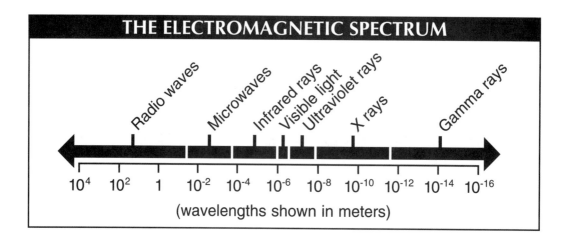

THE ELECTROMAGNETIC SPECTRUM

Radio waves

Microwaves

Infrared rays

Visible light

Ultraviolet rays

X rays

Gamma rays

10^4 10^2 1 10^{-2} 10^{-4} 10^{-6} 10^{-8} 10^{-10} 10^{-12} 10^{-14} 10^{-16}

(wavelengths shown in meters)

Electromagnetic waves are described in terms of their wavelength and frequency. The waves in the electromagnetic spectrum range from short, high-frequency gamma rays to the long, low-frequency radio waves that Marconi would use to revolutionize communications technology.

In the late 1880s, a German scientist named Heinrich Hertz carried out important experiments on radio waves, a form of electromagnetic radiation. Hertz was able to produce and detect the waves that Maxwell had believed to exist. He found that radio waves did move at the speed of light and, like light, could be redirected and reflected. These experiments proved that the mysterious new waves not only traveled through wire, but they also radiated outward from the wire and into space. Therefore, energy could travel through air at the speed of light and people could control this lightning-fast energy! After reading about Hertz's famous experiments, scientists everywhere began to explore the possible uses of electromagnetic radiation.

When Hertz died in 1894, his funeral notice in the newspaper was read by a 20-year-old Italian engineering student named Guglielmo Marconi. The son of an Irish mother and an Italian father, Guglielmo had grown up on the family's estate in northern Italy. He had been a poor student but had tinkered with machines and conducted scientific experiments since his early boyhood. Young Guglielmo had developed a keen interest in the mysterious properties of electricity and electromagnetic waves. Like many students, he was also unsure about his future and was under great pressure from his parents to find a respectable career. His father thought that his son's dabbling in science was a waste of time.

The article about Heinrich Hertz had included a description of his famous experiments. As Marconi read about Hertz's work, he was struck by the idea that electromagnetic waves could possibly carry messages through the air, just as they carried messages along a wire.

Such a "wireless" system would have many advantages over the conventional telegraph. Wireless operators could send their Morse-code messages to and from moving ships and trains. Large cities could be linked with remote, uninhabited corners of the globe. The network of telegraph wires, which could easily be cut or damaged by storms, would become obsolete. Instead, people all over the world could communicate with each other—on a puff of air!

Annie Jameson Marconi with her small son Guglielmo

THE BREAKTHROUGH

To test his idea, Marconi set up a small laboratory in the attic of his family home near Bologna, Italy. At first, he simply tried to duplicate Hertz's experiments. Marconi set up two coiled wires and placed their ends on either side of a short space called a spark gap. When he applied a burst of electricity to the wire, an electric spark crossed the gap between the two wires, sending electromagnetic waves through the air. As Hertz had demonstrated, the waves produced at the "transmitter" also created a spark at the small "receiver."

Marconi wanted to find a practical use for this energy that traveled without a wire. His first inspiration was to add telegraph instruments to the circuit

Marconi used an apparatus similar to this transformer for his spark-gap experiments.

to turn this traveling energy—radio waves—into a form of communication. Once he had sent this "wireless communication" across a room, Marconi tried to increase the distance the waves could travel. To strengthen their force, he placed a small, curved metal reflector behind the transmitter. The waves bounced against the plate and traveled toward the receiver with greater strength.

Marconi also made changes at the receiving end. The most popular detector of electrical activity in a wireless electric circuit was known as a coherer. It was a small glass tube partially filled with iron filings. Wires connected to an antenna were attached to metal rods inserted at each end of the tube. When a burst of electrical energy was picked up by the receiving antenna, it temporarily magnetized the filings, packing them closer together and completing the electric circuit. This dramatically reduced the electrical resistance within the device and produced a measurable increase in the flow of current throughout the entire circuit.

antenna: an apparatus for sending and receiving electromagnetic waves

electric resistance: the opposition of a substance to current passing through it, weakening the electric current

Marconi wired the clapper from an ordinary doorbell into his receiving circuit. Now every time a dot or a dash—a short or longer interruption in the electric circuit—caused the filings to cohere (or stick together), the doorbell clapper would tap the side of the coherer. Marconi further improved the device by heating the glass before sealing it to create a partial vacuum and by using nickel and silver filings instead of iron. He also attached an inker and paper to his circuit so there would be a visible record of the dots and dashes.

Soon Marconi moved his equipment out of the attic and into the family vegetable garden. He was no longer interested in transmissions that could travel only across his yard. To be commercially successful, this project had to be able to operate over long distances.

Marconi attached metal plates to the antennas of both the transmitter and the receiver. He soon found that if he raised one of the transmitting antennas high into the air and buried the other half of the transmitting circuit in the ground, he could send wireless messages for hundreds of meters and over hills and uneven terrain. It was time to patent and sell his invention.

Marconi first approached the Italian Ministry of Posts and Telegraphs. The officials at this government office, however, were quite satisfied with their traditional methods of telegraph communication by wire.

When the Italian government showed no interest in her son's invention, Annie Jameson decided to take him and his wireless-telegraph system to Great Britain. Jameson family connections there won mother and son access to important officials. A promotional genius, Marconi convinced these government and military leaders that wireless technology would not only be especially valuable for military communications, but it would also have tremendous commercial prospects. Furthermore, Marconi argued, unlike systems with less sensitive coherers and antenna arrangements, his system would make wireless communication practical.

Marconi demonstrated his device on the roof of the London general post office for English patent officials. In 1896 and 1897, he staged a series of demonstrations of his wireless equipment on Salisbury Plain in southern England. The officials were astonished to hear signals that had traveled distances of more than four miles through the air. Marconi patented his wireless equipment in June 1896; by 1897, the device was sending messages from the coast of England to islands in the Bristol Channel nine miles away.

After learning of Marconi's successful tests, Italian and British military leaders sought him out. Wireless equipment, Marconi explained, was a perfect way to transmit signals from ship to ship and from ship to shore. The wireless would also give any cruiser or destroyer a great advantage during a battle, when smoke and confusion often scramble important messages sent by flags. To demonstrate, Marconi loaned his equipment to British ships engaged in military exercises and mock battles. During the tests, the ships equipped with the wireless always emerged victorious.

An astute businessman, Marconi and some members of his mother's family established the Wireless Telegraph and Signal Company in 1897. (The company was renamed Marconi's Wireless Telegraph Company in 1899.) At the age of 23, Marconi was in control of a business worth £100,000 (about $10 million in today's money). Anyone who wished to use Marconi's device had to pay his company a licensing fee. Marconi's invention—and his

Twenty-two-year-old Marconi poses with his first wireless telegraph in 1896.

abilities to promote it—would make him one of the world's most powerful men.

The Italian navy soon installed Marconi's wireless equipment on its ships. Over the next few years, the Wireless Telegraph and Signal Company also set up a maritime (sea-based) wireless service in England, building permanent wireless stations at Poole on the southern coast and on the Isle of Wight in the English Channel. Marconi designed 100-foot transmitting and receiving towers for the stations, which used Morse code to send weather reports and to receive distress signals from ships at sea.

To publicize his wireless further, Marconi used it to cover yacht races in the English Channel in

1898. Riding a tugboat equipped with his device, he transmitted results of the races to a shore station. The information was then sent to the Dublin *Daily Express* by telephone, and the newspaper posted the results outside its offices. Newspapers throughout England soon began to use Marconi's system and praised its potential in numerous articles.

During the next year, Marconi staged the same demonstration in the United States. Off New York Harbor, where the popular America's Cup Yacht Races were being held, wireless operators stood by on observation ships to send racing results to the public. For the first time, American yacht-racing fans received instantaneous news about the progress of their favorite teams.

Commercial steamship lines crossing the Atlantic Ocean were the first civilian companies to employ wireless technology. Passenger and cargo ships used Marconi's sets to radio their positions to shore stations and to provide a message service for passengers. Eventually, Marconi also brought his invention to stations on dry land. The Marconi-gram began to replace the telegram because wireless messages proved to be easier to handle and more dependable. The wireless didn't rely on long wire networks that could be interrupted by bad weather or breaks in the line.

In the next few years, the wireless telegraph went through several improvements. Marconi continually searched for ways to produce and send stronger signals and also sought to build equipment capable of handling as many messages as possible.

wavelength: the distance between the peak of one wave and the peak of the next corresponding wave

This Marconi tuner was built between 1910 and 1916.

An innovation by British inventor Oliver Lodge greatly helped Marconi in this quest.

In 1897, Lodge had come up with the idea of sending electrical signals of a single wavelength and frequency through the atmosphere. Receiving stations could "tune" their equipment to these radio waves, which made it possible for receiving equipment to detect a much clearer signal. Because a wireless station could monitor several frequencies at once, more than one message could be sent and received at the same time. Marconi soon adapted this idea to his own equipment.

By 1900, wireless technology had advanced so far that operators were able to send signals several hundred miles across land or sea. Marconi now felt his equipment was ready for a difficult test: sending a message across the Atlantic Ocean from Europe to North America. With the help of prominent scientist J. A. Fleming, he built a new and more powerful transmitting station at the coastal town of Poldhu in southwestern England's Cornwall region.

For months, Marconi prepared for the first transatlantic wireless transmission. Several times, high winds brought down his antennas, and poor weather constantly interfered with the transmission of signals. Finally, on December 12, 1901, at a receiving station in Newfoundland, Canada, Marconi heard the faint Morse-code signal for "S"—three short dots—that had traveled nearly 3,000 miles from his station in Cornwall. Wireless messages could cross the wide Atlantic!

THE RESULT

Wireless-telegraph transmission made Marconi an international celebrity. He now spent much of his time traveling around the world in his private yacht, demonstrating new innovations in wireless technology and meeting with scientists and political and military leaders.

At the same time, many other inventors were trying to improve Marconi's basic design. In 1904, Marconi's colleague J. A. Fleming replaced the coherer by applying a finding made earlier by Thomas Edison. While working on his electric light

Marconi (standing) and an assistant read the telegraph tape shortly after the successful wireless transmission across the Atlantic Ocean.

English electrical engineer J. A. Fleming (1849-1945) was knighted by the British government in 1929 in honor of his scientific discoveries.

bulb in 1880, Edison had discovered that if he put a metal plate inside the bulb and applied a positive charge to it, current would flow from the lit filament to the charged plate, even if the filament and the plate were not in contact with each other. This "Edison Effect" was the basis for Fleming's improved detector, or "Fleming valve." In completing the electrical circuit, the coherer only indicated the presence of electrical activity. The Fleming valve could carry the human voice—and even music!

Within a few years, other inventors were tinkering with the Fleming valve in an attempt to receive a wider range of frequencies. Their goal was to transmit and receive the human voice through the atmosphere. Inventors continued to develop

A 1916 Marconi Mark III receiver owned by industrialist Andrew Mellon

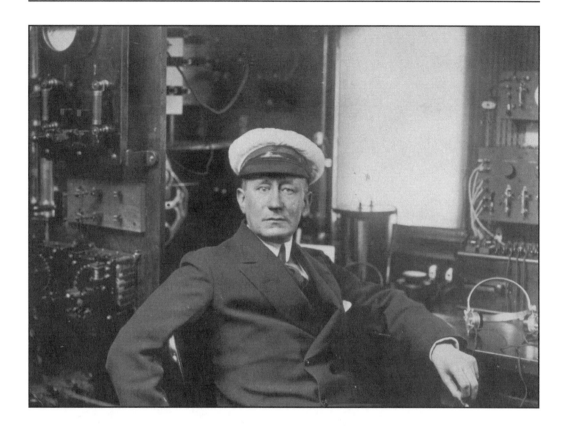

technology that made it possible for radio waves to carry the human voice instead of just the dots and dashes of the Morse code. By the 1920s, commercial radio stations were operating in several U.S. cities.

By the time Marconi died on July 20, 1937, radio was the most popular entertainment and information medium in the world. To honor his passing, all wireless stations observed two minutes of silence. Although inventors and improving technology eventually left Marconi's wireless telegraph behind, the public continued to revere this skillful inventor and businessman as the "Father of the Wireless."

Captain Marconi on his yacht, Elettra, *where he conducted wireless experiments. In 1909, Marconi received the Nobel Prize in Physics.*

CHAPTER SIX

Lee de Forest and Edwin Howard Armstrong and the Radio

The creations of Alexander Graham Bell and Guglielmo Marconi had brought about a new era of instant communication across nations, continents, and oceans by the early twentieth century. The inventor was the new hero of this electronic age, replacing the kings and conquerors of the past. To people living in a suddenly smaller world, it seemed that scientific genius, combined with the mysterious power of electricity, could make any form of communication possible.

Wouldn't it be wonderful, some inventors thought, if people could hear each other's voices over the wireless instead of only the cumbersome and slow dots and dashes of the Morse code? The secret to receiving a human voice over the airwaves lay in a device called the detector. A variety of natural and artificial crystals can "detect" a human voice in the

When he was a college student, Lee de Forest (1873-1961) wrote in his diary, "I must be brilliant, win fame, show the greatness of genius and to no small degree."

The crystal detector received radio signals by blocking out the part of the radio wave that prevented the reception of sound.

Before the inventions of de Forest and Edwin Howard Armstrong, Alexanderson alternators—huge devices as heavy as a semi-truck full of car batteries—were used to generate the power for voice transmission at radio stations.

electromagnetic radiation: energy in the form of traveling waves that results when an electromagnetic field produced by an electric current is disturbed because the current has been altered

complex radio wave. Within months of their 1906 discovery, 10-cent crystal detectors could be purchased by anyone with the curiosity and ingenuity to experiment with them.

Tuning in a radio wave and hearing a feeble voice on a pair of headphones was fine for the amateur experimenter, but for radio to be successful, it had to be loud enough for everyone to hear. The challenge of amplification had not yet been met.

Inventors and other visionaries longed to put voices and music onto the air waves. The answer to the problem of transmitting sound by radio waves would reside in a mysterious little bottle of wires called the de Forest audion. Its inventor was an ambitious misfit named Lee de Forest. The key that unlocked the mysteries of the audion would be turned by the hand of Edwin Howard Armstrong. Because the discoveries of each man depended on the work of the other for their success, Armstrong and de Forest engaged in one of the longest and most bitter legal battles in the history of invention to determine which of them really could claim the title "Father of Radio."

Young Edwin Howard Armstrong shared the fascination with electronics of many children of his generation. After reading about Marconi and other innovators in the field of wireless telegraphy, Armstrong realized that electronic communication was just in its beginning stages. In 1904, at the age of 13, he set out to find new ways of capturing and using radio waves, a form of electromagnetic radiation that Marconi was using in his wireless telegraph.

Edwin Howard Armstrong (1890-1954) poses with his first portable radio during his 1923 honeymoon.

The tiny Fleming valve, only a few inches long, promised to revolutionize wireless technology.

direct current: electric current that flows in one direction

Armstrong grew up in a big, three-story house in Yonkers, a city overlooking the Hudson River not far upstream from New York City. Like Marconi, he set up his own wireless laboratory in the attic of his family's home, assembling a collection of all the latest components necessary to construct the new world of wireless communication. His goal was the goal of many other inventors of the time: to find a way to transmit and receive the human voice with radio waves.

To many inventors, the new Fleming valve offered the possibility of detecting voice transmissions. The Fleming valve and the crystal detector both work on the principle of rectification. A rectifier allows current to flow in one direction only. Radio waves, and the information they carry, are made up of alternating currents. This means the waves rapidly change from positive to negative current and back again thousands of times each second.

Once these radio waves are picked up and tuned in by an antenna, they need to be converted into the pulses that the human ear can perceive. Sensitive rectifiers such as the Fleming valve and the crystal detector were the first components capable of such action.

One of the inventors who saw the promise of the Fleming valve was Lee de Forest. The son of a clergyman in Alabama, de Forest had studied at the Sheffield Scientific School, part of the prestigious Yale University. Ambitious and tireless, he spent much of his time tinkering with gadgets and experimenting with ideas developed by other inventors.

In 1906, de Forest added a wire grid between the filament and metal plate of the Fleming valve. When the device was hooked up to a receiving antenna, this grid greatly strengthened the electrical current passing through the valve. At a certain point, de Forest believed, the magnified signal produced by the device would be able to carry a human voice.

De Forest called his modified Fleming valve the audion. He wasn't quite sure why it worked, but he quickly patented the device. In his patent application, de Forest predicted that his invention could be used to strengthen telephone signals by magnifying the current along telephone lines in a series of relays.

Although the audion worked as a telephone relay, it still had some serious technical problems. At a certain amplification, the product would create a loud, irregular howl, which was the product of its own waves. Fed back into the audion's circuit and thus repeated again and again, these waves created a screeching interference. Try as he might, de Forest was unable to figure out the source of this howl or to eliminate it.

In addition to the howl in his audion, de Forest was running into other problems with some earlier inventions. Rival inventors claimed that he had simply copied their radio technology, adding small changes and then patenting the devices under different names.

De Forest lost his first of many major patent battles in 1906 after three years in court. In 1903, Canadian scientist Reginald Fessenden had produced

De Forest had high hopes for his audion, writing in his diary that he believed it would solve all his personal and financial problems.

feedback: the repeated reflowing of an electrical signal back into a circuit to increase its strength

interference: the prevention of clear broadcast signals

Reginald Fessenden (1866-1932) was the first person to transmit sound waves over the wireless when, on December 24, 1906, he sent Christmas greetings and music to the startled crew members of ships off the Massachusetts coast.

a new and effective detector that he called a liquid barretter. After seeing Fessenden's invention, de Forest produced the spade detector, which he designed in a way that disguised its similarity to Fessenden's barretter.

When Fessenden won his patent suit against de Forest in 1906, de Forest was prohibited from manufacturing his similar device. But de Forest's legal troubles were far from over. After patenting the audion tube the following year, he began to stage demonstrations of its broadcasting capabilities. These included a 1908 performance from the Eiffel Tower in Paris and a few moments of a New York Metropolitan Opera concert by Enrico Caruso in 1910. These displays of the wonders of the audion were put to a stop in 1914, when the Marconi Company took Lee de Forest to court, claiming that the inventor had stolen its Fleming-valve design in making the device. De Forest lost this legal battle as well, and the court ordered him to stop selling the audion.

De Forest's public demonstrations led to other brushes with the law. From 1906 to 1913, he set up several companies to take advantage of the intense interest in what was called "radio telephony." After a demonstration, company directors would sell stock to the public to raise capital. But the companies misled the stockholders about the potential success of their products. After de Forest and the other directors had pocketed more than three-quarters of the money invested in their schemes, the fledgling businesses went bankrupt and closed down.

Although de Forest was acquitted, two of the other directors were convicted of fraud charges early in 1914.

As de Forest and the other inventors sparred in the courtroom and sought monetary rewards for their work, Edwin Howard Armstrong quietly began experimenting with the Fleming valve in his attic laboratory in Yonkers. In 1911, the young man acquired his first audion tube and brought it to the laboratories of New York's Columbia University, where he was studying electrical engineering. He tested and retested the audion, determined to find out exactly how it worked.

De Forest's audion was sold mounted on a panel with hookups for headphones and power.

THE BREAKTHROUGH

Armstrong carefully measured the electrical current hundreds of times as it flowed between filament and plate within the audion. He concluded that the audion was essentially a way of moving electrons from one place to another. From this observation, Armstrong reasoned that he could take the current that was traveling from the plate to the headphones and feed it back into the signal that was flowing through the audion. By regenerating the electric current in this manner, the current should amplify itself as the charge to the grid increased the power flowing from filament to plate.

On September 22, 1912, Armstrong was finally ready to test his new circuit, which he had strengthened by adding two more wire coils to the antenna.

electron: a particle in the atom that has a negative electrical charge

A model of Armstrong's regenerative circuit—a feedback loop for the audion

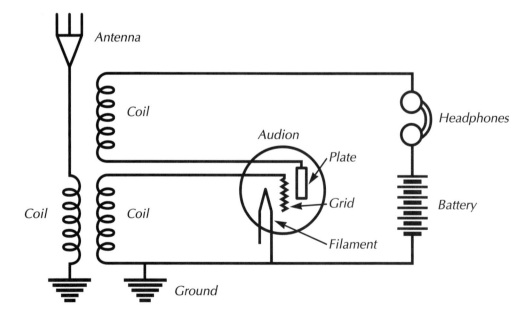

When power began to flow and feed back through the audion, the sound of Morse code came roaring through the headphones, louder and clearer than ever before.

At certain power levels, the feedback loop produced a strange hissing sound. Armstrong realized that the audion tube was oscillating and producing its own radio waves. The young man had accidentally discovered that his radio receiver was also a powerful radio transmitter!

oscillate: to switch back and forth from alternate extremes

Throughout the winter, Armstrong made adjustments to what he called the "regenerative circuit." With it, he could hear wireless signals from all over the United States as well as Europe. But without enough money to apply for a patent (his father refused to help him until he finished college), the inventor had to keep his regenerative circuit a secret.

In 1913, Armstrong finally graduated from Columbia University. As promised, his father made him a loan, and Armstrong filed for a patent on his regenerative receiving circuit that October. In December, he filed another patent application for a regenerative transmitter.

Now ready to introduce his regenerative circuit to the world, Armstrong began giving demonstrations to audiences at the Institute of Radio Engineers and the Radio Club of America. He cautiously kept the tubes and wires in a closed box so no one could copy and reproduce his circuitry. One night in 1913, a very curious Lee de Forest watched Armstrong's demonstration, wishing he could examine the apparatus Armstrong kept out of sight.

Armstrong and de Forest were not the only wireless inventors of the time. In 1912, the U.S. Patent Office awarded 350 patents for radio technology.

THE RESULT

Soon amateurs across the United States were using Armstrong's regenerative circuit to broadcast voice and music. Small radio stations sprang up, carrying informal broadcasts. Inventors kept trying to improve the regenerative circuit enough to file for a patent on an entirely new device.

In March 1914, Lee de Forest filed his own patent application for a device he called the "ultra audion." The U.S. Patent Office decided the invention was too similar to Armstrong's to be patented, but de Forest continued to amend and resubmit his application until it was accepted. Then, in 1915, de Forest publicly claimed to have discovered the regenerative circuit.

De Forest and Armstrong now began to spar over the rights to the regenerative circuit. Their legal battles heated up in 1920 after Armstrong sold his patent to Westinghouse and de Forest sold his to the American Telephone and Telegraph Company (AT&T). Two different corporations now owned the regenerative circuit, and two different men were claiming to be its inventor.

De Forest argued that his audion telephone relay and his ultra audion were the first devices to use a regenerative circuit. What he did not mention, however, was that he had been unaware of the audion's capability as a radio transmitter—and unfamiliar with the regenerative circuit—until after Armstrong had applied for his patents in 1913. Armstrong, meanwhile, maintained that even though

he had based his work on de Forest's audion design, his experiments in the autumn of 1912 had produced the first practical radio transmitter.

It took 20 years of litigation to settle the dispute between Edwin Howard Armstrong and Lee de Forest. Federal court justices, who consistently failed to understand the technical aspects of the case, ruled first for Armstrong, then for de Forest, and then for Armstrong again. Finally, the second time the case reached the U.S. Supreme Court, Lee de Forest was named the true "Father of Radio" on May 21, 1934.

In the midst of legal battles over the rights to the radio, the new device made its way into businesses and homes. By 1923, more than 550 radio stations broadcast to over 400,000 radios.

Lee de Forest at work in his Los Angeles laboratory. Most historians of science believe the Supreme Court failed to understand the technical aspects of the case and as a result made a bad decision in de Forest's favor.

By the late 1920s, Armstrong had moved on to the problem of radio interference. David Sarnoff of the Radio Corporation of America (RCA) had challenged him to create a new system to eliminate this annoying static.

Unlike most scientists in the radio industry at the time, Armstrong thought that broadcasting radio waves over a wide band of frequencies—a system called frequency modulation (FM)—would decrease the static. The problem with amplitude modulation (AM)—the traditional method of radio transmission that varied the height of the waves—was that it was impossible to eliminate static from the sound because AM radio waves and static were too similar in structure. Frequency modulation avoided the static by broadcasting different signals with slightly varying frequencies of radio waves. In 1933, Armstrong patented the first FM transmitters and receivers.

amplitude: the greatest height or strength reached by a wave

As soon as he received his patent, Armstrong demonstrated his FM system to his old friend David Sarnoff at RCA. Although Armstrong would repeatedly demonstrate FM's superior transmission to RCA's executives and engineers, RCA stalled on buying the patent rights because Sarnoff believed that television—which RCA was feverishly developing—would make radio obsolete.

Armstrong's relationship with David Sarnoff quickly deteriorated when the RCA executive took de Forest's side in the radio dispute because his company now owned the rights to de Forest's invention.

When Armstrong realized that RCA was not going to come through with an offer, he held his own public demonstrations of his FM system. Then, in the spring of 1937, he began to build an FM radio station in Alpine, New Jersey. Impressed by Armstrong's "staticless radio," General Electric and

Armstrong's radio station, W2XMN Alpine, made its first broadcast with a clear FM signal on July 18, 1939.

Many people see Edwin Howard Armstrong as a symbol of the lone inventor fighting the greedy world of big business. Patriotic and fair-minded, he had allowed the government to use his FM radios without paying royalties during World War II.

other companies paid him for licenses to produce FM systems for sale.

In 1940, finally recognizing the advantages of FM systems, Sarnoff offered Armstrong $1 million for the right to use his technology. Still furious over RCA's earlier treatment of him, Armstrong rejected his former friend's offer.

When RCA began to use the FM system in their televisions in 1947, claiming that the technology had been developed by company engineers, another legal battle loomed for Armstrong. He sued RCA for patent infringement in 1948 and spent the next five years trying to defend his right to his own invention.

By late 1953, Edwin Howard Armstrong was broke and disheartened. Haunted by his failures and setbacks, he jumped to his death from the window of his New York City apartment on February 1, 1954. Following her husband's suicide, Marion Armstrong continued his litigation and she achieved some vindication by eventually winning court settlements from every company—including RCA—that had infringed on his patents.

Today's radios use diode detectors and transistor amplifiers. Both are direct descendants of the 1906 crystal detector. Perhaps if what is known now had been known then, the entire era of the Fleming valve and its offspring as well as the long and bitter court battles between Armstrong, de Forest, and Marconi might have been avoided.

A household fixture since the 1920s, radio is more popular than ever. And television, which began to dominate the communications market at the time of Armstrong's death, uses radio waves to transmit images as well as sound. Harnessed by Marconi, de Forest, and Armstrong, the once mysterious radio waves have become the basis of the modern communications industry.

As this July 1922 cover of Science and Invention *magazine shows, it didn't take radio innovators long to imagine television transmission using the new radio technology.*

CHAPTER SEVEN

Philo Farnsworth and the Television

At the same time that Alexander Graham Bell's early telephones were carrying the human voice over a network of electrified wires, a new discovery was inaugurating the age of image broadcasting. Even though working televisions did not become a part of people's everyday lives until after the end of World War II in 1945, scientists by that time had already been experimenting with television technology for more than 70 years.

In 1873, an electrician for a telegraph company reported that the chemical element selenium had decreased resistance to electrical current when it was exposed to light. Excited inventors now wondered whether images could be sent electronically by manipulating light and shade. Alexander Graham Bell himself raised this possibility when he proposed using selenium cells in a "photophone."

Although many inventors suggested ideas for facsimile machines and "electric telescopes" that

Philo Farnsworth at age 24 in 1930, the year he received a patent for his electronic television. In later years, he would not allow his children to watch television because he thought the programs were dreadful.

made use of the photoelectric properties of the selenium cell, no one had come up with a way to scan an image for transmission. Then, in 1884, German scientist Paul Nipkow designed the mechanical-disk image-scanner television. Although he was never able to build the machine, his plan was detailed and workable. His design consisted of a large disk with a number of small holes arranged in a spiral pattern. When the operator spun the disk, the holes passed one after another over a lit-up image, tracing out a series of horizontal lines, each slightly lower than the previous one.

All photographic images are made up of tiny dots. The more dots per inch in the photograph, the sharper the image will be. The mechanical-disk image scanner employed a similar concept. It transmitted images a line at a time (the line was drawn by the hole's sweep) as quickly as possible. Light from the image passed through the holes and, line by line, was guided by lenses and mirrors through a selenium cell. The darker areas of the original image produced a weaker signal in the light-sensitive cell, and the lighter areas created a stronger signal. The cell thus translated the light into varying electronic signals, which were then sent over a wire to a receiver.

At the receiving end, the electronic signals were reconverted to light—which varied in intensity according to the strength of the signal—and then were passed through another spinning disk. As the disk spun, the image was re-created, line by line, on a small screen. The result was a faint image of

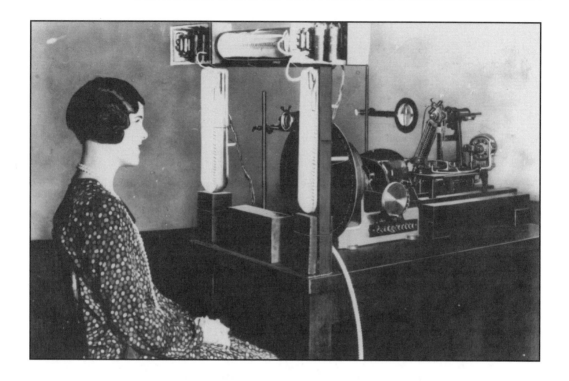

the object at the receiving end—and the invention of mechanical television.

Several people were experimenting with Nipkow's mechanical image-scanning systems by the 1920s. American Charles Francis Jenkins and Scottish inventor John L. Baird nipped at each other's heels in their race to send televised pictures. Jenkins sent the first "radio photograph," as he called it, on May 19, 1922. Three years later, Baird used his mechanical scanner to transmit an image of a Maltese cross, while Jenkins transmitted a moving image—a slowly rotating windmill—a distance of five miles. Jenkins called his mechanical-television system "radio vision."

A woman waits to be scanned by a 1930 mechanical-television system. The bright lights in front of the disk help to provide the clearest image possible. As the disk spins and scans the woman's image line by line, the lens behind the disk focuses the image on a selenium cell to be translated into an electronic signal for transmission.

Charles Francis Jenkins (right) with his mechanical television. He called his work "the development of radio as a service to the eye."

Because the mechanical-television system scanned images in a 60-line sequence (modern televisions use 525-line images) and was limited in speed, the resulting picture was choppy and blurred.

By the late 1920s, the British Broadcasting Corporation (BBC) was making experimental broadcasts with Baird's system. In the United States, a tiny audience, equipped with mechanical-disk receivers, tuned in to the first television programs.

In 1931, the Columbia Broadcasting System (CBS) in New York City also began experimenting with a mechanical-television system. Jenkins, Baird, and others were sure that the mechanical scanner would soon provide images sharp enough for commercial broadcasting. But they were wrong.

Television's future was electronic, not mechanical, as Philo T. Farnsworth realized quite early in his life. Born on August 19, 1906, to a Mormon family living in a log cabin near Beaver City, Utah, Philo enjoyed a natural talent for tinkering. At age six, he announced that he was going to be an inventor.

When Philo was 12, the family moved north to the Snake River Valley in Idaho. In their new house, Philo finally had access to electricity. Neighbors were amazed when the boy built an electric-powered washing machine from an electric battery and an old, hand-cranked washing basin. Stacks of science magazines Philo found in the attic soon hooked him on electronics. In addition to reading about the latest theories and inventions, he took advanced chemistry in high school.

Because radios and telephones could transmit sound electronically, Philo figured a machine should be able to transmit images in a similar manner. But he realized that mechanical systems would never be fast enough to transmit a high-quality image. Then one day while plowing a field, Philo wondered whether an image could be scanned electronically in rows, just as a farmer drives back and forth along his rows of corn. Unlike mechanical scanning, electronic scanning could be performed almost instantly, creating a much sharper picture.

Philo imagined the design of an electronic image-transmitting machine. The teenager's concept became the framework for the "image dissector" he would develop later. His plan called for a selenium cell to be placed inside a vacuum tube that was coated with a light-sensitive substance. A lens would focus an image onto the tube's light-sensitive interior surface. Like the mechanical-disk image scanner, Philo's device would scan line by line, but the electronic system would be far more effective because the scanning would be executed at the speed of light. The selenium cell would convert the image into an electrical signal that would be transmitted electronically to the receiver.

In a cathode-ray tube at the receiving end, a filament would give off the stream of electrons it had received from the transmitter. The cathode-ray tube would then convert the electronic signal back into an image. As in the mechanical system, the selenium cell would reproduce the darker and lighter areas by varying the electronic signal according to the level of light. If everything worked as planned, the rectangular screen would then glow with the received image—not just dots and dashes, not just words and music, but images of life itself could be sent instantaneously over long distances!

But Philo was only 15 years old. He didn't have enough money to experiment with his ideas, and it would be many years before he could.

Philo's family moved from Idaho to Provo, Utah, where he graduated from high school. After a stint in the navy, Philo returned to Utah when his father died. While taking classes at Brigham Young University, the 18-year-old delivered radios for a furniture shop to help support his family.

A break finally came for the would-be inventor when he met professional fundraisers George Everson and Leslie Gorrell. They hired Farnsworth, who quickly impressed them as a capable and very

cathode-ray tube: a vacuum tube into which a cathode emits electrons that are in turn passed through an anode and then focused on a glowing screen

filament: a thinly spun wire

smart worker. Sensing that he might have an opportunity to return to his research, Farnsworth explained to them his television device and his need for money. The two men knew little about electronics—few people did in the mid-1920s—but Farnsworth's enthusiasm prompted them to invest their life's savings—$6,000—in the 19-year-old's dream. They believed that if commercial-quality broadcasting were possible, selling it to the public would create huge profits.

With Gorrell and Everson, Philo Farnsworth moved to Los Angeles to set up his first laboratory. On the eve of his departure, the young man married Elma Gardner in a Mormon service. In the couple's rented duplex, with the window shades always down, he and Elma (who had studied mathematics and electronics) worked to build and assemble the needed equipment. The newlyweds and their financial backers crafted tools, wound wire coils, and purchased equipment they could not make themselves.

After the system exploded during the first trial experiment, Farnsworth's lab was out of funds. Unable to continue his support, Everson introduced Farnsworth to three wealthy San Francisco bankers: W. W. Crocker, James Fagan, and Jesse McCargar. The three men asked electrical engineers to study Farnsworth's designs and then decided to put up $25,000. McCargar saw the potential in Farnworth's work. "This is not engineering we are backing," he said, "it is invention." Farnsworth moved to San Francisco to be near his investors and once again began working on his television.

Neighbors of the Farnsworths called the police on the suspicion that the couple were keeping their shades closed because they were illegally producing alcohol during Prohibition.

THE BREAKTHROUGH

After setting up his new workshop in San Francisco, Farnsworth spent months trying to find the right materials for his electronic-television system. The tubes had to be airtight, and the wire coils had to be carefully adjusted to create the electromagnetic fields that controlled the scanning. For two years, Farnsworth and his assistants ran hundreds of tests.

Finally, in 1928, Farnsworth had a working transmitter and receiver. The receiver's screen was a small piece of smooth glass about four inches square.

Farnsworth (right) with engineer Albert Mann. The inventor's image dissector that scanned images line by line electronically eliminated the mechanical system's scanning disk.

The bankers gathered around the receiver grumbled about when they were "going to see some dollars in this thing."

While they watched, a faint and blurry image came through on the receiving screen. As if to assure his investors that there would be money in this machine, the inventor had transmitted the image of a dollar sign! Later, Farnsworth was able to send moving images of burning cigarettes and a film of a hockey game—the world's first sportscast. At least in the laboratory, the Farnsworth television system seemed to work.

As his television was gaining publicity during the next two years, Farnsworth continued to test and refine the system. Renowned scientists and inventors—Guglielmo Marconi, whose wireless telegraph marked the beginning of the radio age; Lee de Forest, one of the radio's inventors; and future physics Nobel prizewinner Ernest O. Lawrence—were among those who visited the Farnsworth lab. Two famous movie actors, Douglas Fairbanks and Mary Pickford, also came. Farnsworth had long been using clips from one of their films, *The Taming of the Shrew*, for his television demonstrations.

But Farnsworth soon faced tough competition from Vladimir Zworykin, an inventor working in the Radio Corporation of America (RCA) laboratories. A Russian immigrant, Zworykin was hired in 1930 by David Sarnoff of RCA to produce his own electronic television. Zworykin visited Farnsworth's lab that year and listened intently as Farnsworth showed him how each part of his television system

Like Farnsworth's investors, we see whole images on television because of a phenomenon called persistence of vision. Even though a televised image is actually made up of hundreds of lines, these lines appear in such quick succession that our eyes instead perceive a complete picture.

worked. Farnsworth had hoped RCA would offer to back his work; instead, Zworykin used Farnsworth's equipment as a guide in designing his own.

Both Zworykin and Farnsworth realized that mechanical-disk scanners would never be useful for public broadcasting because the disks could not scan the 60-line images quickly enough to produce a good picture. An electronic system, using electrons that moved at the speed of light, was the only way to send the image signal fast enough to create a quality image.

After building a replica of Farnsworth's television, Zworykin devised two ingenious new television tubes, being careful not to break patent law by making them too similar to the Farnsworth model. For a transmitter, he created the iconoscope. This device held a small, rectangular plate coated with light-sensitive material. A lens focused an object in front of the iconoscope tube onto the plate, storing the image as varying electric charges. An electron beam then scanned the plate and transformed the stored electrical charges into varying electrical impulses that could be sent to a receiver electronically and translated back into the light and dark areas of the image.

At the receiving end of the system, Zworykin built a kinescope, or television camera tube. In the kinescope, the electrical signal powered another beam of electrons, which swept the end of the tube. The electron beam built the image by sweeping across the tube's screen in a series of horizontal lines that, line by line, created a picture on the tube. The greater the number of lines, the sharper the picture.

Vladimir Zworykin (1889-1982) poses with his later RCA Image Orthicon camera tube. Developed in 1946, it was 100 times more sensitive than any previous television camera tube.

At the same time Zworykin was busy in the RCA laboratories, Farnsworth was perfecting his working model so that he could apply for a patent. He called his device an "image dissector" because it dissected the image into lines and then reassembled it again, line by line. In August 1930, the U.S. Patent Office awarded Farnsworth two patents for his television system.

Disappointed that Farnsworth had beaten his company in the television race, RCA president David

Sarnoff began negotiations for the rights to Philo Farnsworth's image dissector. But Farnsworth turned down his offer of $100,000 (almost $1 million in today's money).

Instead, in 1931 Farnsworth signed a secret licensing agreement with the Philco Radio Corporation, the largest manufacturer of radios in the country, and moved his family and laboratory to Philadelphia. When RCA learned that Philco was testing television transmission, RCA threatened to deny radio licensing to Philco, and the company had to cancel its contract with Farnsworth.

Farnsworth decided to remain in Philadelphia, and he opened the Farnsworth Radio and Television Company in 1933. He had hoped to develop television for commercial use on his own, but his company did not have enough money to popularize commercial television. To sell television sets, Farnsworth's company would have to produce televisions cheaply enough to make them affordable. It would also have to create quality news and entertainment programs to convince people that they needed television sets. Farnsworth hoped to license his patents to other companies to raise money for this huge venture.

But RCA's Sarnoff was not going to allow this competition. In 1934, the company filed an interference with Farnsworth's television patents, arguing that Zworykin had created electronic television in 1923. Although Zworykin had, in fact, filed for a patent for electronic television in 1923, there was no evidence that he had built a working system. Farnsworth won this patent battle, partly because of

Zworykin's iconoscope had a mechanism that strengthened the image signal by storing the light energy it received.

testimony from one of his high school teachers, who produced a sketch of an electronic television that his star student had drawn for him in 1922.

Beating RCA did not bring Farnsworth any closer to funding his dream of commercial television. But in the summer of 1934, he finally had the opportunity to introduce his machine when the prestigious Franklin Institute held a two-week series of public demonstrations of Farnsworth's system at the height of the tourist season. Thousands crowded into the institute's auditorium to watch the demonstration. Farnsworth even put audience members on television. People excitedly pointed to images of themselves as they walked through the door.

Newspapers around the United States described the live performances by musicians, dancers, and animals that were televised under the hot lights required for the transmission of the images.

When officials at the British Broadcasting Corporation (BBC) heard about the new television, they acted quickly. The BBC had been broadcasting with the mechanical system developed by John L. Baird, but the company invited Farnsworth to London to demonstrate his electronic television.

After witnessing the Farnsworth system, Baird himself realized that his disk scanner had become obsolete. The BBC prepared to install an electronic system, and Baird paid $50,000 for the right to use the Farnsworth patents. Soon inventors and engineers in France, Germany, England, and Japan were hard at work trying to develop commercial television. It had taken 13 years and more than $1 million to achieve a commercially viable television system.

Farnsworth in his laboratory in 1938 with an improved version of the image dissector camera tube. Two years earlier, European technicians had used his system to broadcast the 1936 Olympic Games in Berlin, Germany.

THE RESULT

Television had a slow beginning in the United States. Although CBS had established regular programming with the Jenkins mechanical system, the network was unprofitable, and CBS closed down television broadcasting in February 1933. In Philadelphia, Farnsworth opened an experimental television station, W3XPF, in the summer of 1936, and a number of other companies also started stations. But the Federal Communications Commission (FCC) had not developed any standards for the broadcasting media, so each company's televisions could only receive transmissions from its own station. These limited viewing options—as well as a lack of cash during the Great Depression—kept audiences tuned to their radio sets.

Frustrated by his lack of success in launching commercial television, Philo Farnsworth became depressed and began drinking heavily. He moved with his family to Maine, where he built a cabin and tried to forget television and the death of one of his young children a few years earlier.

At the 1939 World's Fair, it was RCA and not Farnsworth's company that presented television to the world. "Now we add sight to sound," David Sarnoff announced, and his company touted itself as the inventor of television. RCA arranged for President Franklin D. Roosevelt to deliver a speech on the air—the first televised appearance by an American president—which RCA transmitted to several hundred television sets in New York City.

Many historians inaccurately state that RCA's World's Fair booth was the first public demonstration of electronic television, but Farnsworth's presentations at the Franklin Institute had occurred in 1934—five years before that!

Millions of people from around the world came to New York City to see the newest inventions at the 1939 World's Fair.

Farnsworth won his patent battle with RCA in October 1939, several months after the end of the World's Fair.

After the fair, RCA was finally forced to pay Farnsworth royalties to use his system—the first time the company had paid a licensing fee. But in 1941, when the United States entered World War II, the government ordered television factories to convert to weapons production, and most broadcasting stations closed for the duration of the war. Farnsworth's most important patents expired in 1947, so World War II meant the end of his dream. Although television became the world's most popular medium of mass entertainment in the 1950s and 1960s, the invention brought little fame to Philo Farnsworth.

Farnsworth instead turned to other projects, creating an electronic microscope and a gastroscope, a device that transmitted images of the stomach. Another Farnsworth machine—the predecessor of the modern facsimile, or fax, machine—could send a picture of a letter or document over a telephone line. The inventor spent most of the last two decades of his life studying nuclear fusion, which he believed would solve the world's energy problems.

Television has gone through many changes in the last half century. Color television was introduced to the public in 1954, and, in the 1970s, the number of television stations expanded rapidly as the spread of cable systems improved television reception and offered more specialized programming. By the 1990s, satellite broadcasting systems were bringing an even greater spectrum of stations and programming into people's homes.

A new revolution in television is on the horizon for the early twenty-first century. To produce images as clear and as sharp as real life, engineers have perfected high-definition television (HDTV) that uses digital signals to send images with at least twice the number of scanning lines as traditional television systems. As in the 1930s, the obstacle is the system's high cost. But, beginning in 1999, HDTV will likely be available to the public, and it is scheduled by 2006 to replace completely the television systems descended from Philo Farnsworth's image dissector.

Although World War II ended in 1945, Farnsworth did not have the money to fund large-scale production of his television system in the two years remaining on his patent.

Philo Farnsworth died in 1970, forgotten by the public.

The Information Superhighway

People call the end of the twentieth century "The Information Age." A revolution in communications has led to an explosion of information available at the touch of a button. The power of the computer to store and process data has become accessible to more and more people through the Internet system of linked computer networks worldwide. This system, which is now used by millions of businesses and individuals for communicating, research, and advertising, was born in the 1960s as a military project to develop a communications system that could withstand catastrophic warfare.

At that time, the United States and the Soviet Union were fighting a "Cold War," a tense global rivalry between the two superpowers that threatened to break out into World War III. Both sides readied for the conflict by building weapons, training armies, and preparing to defend themselves.

Leaders on both sides knew a war could result in a nuclear confrontation. An exchange of nuclear

In the early years of the twenty-first century, the Teledesic Corporation intends to launch hundreds of satellites into space to make the Internet available everywhere in the world.

This atomic bomb explosion over Nagasaki, Japan, in August 1945 revealed the power of nuclear weapons.

Paul Baran of the RAND Corporation

weapons would destroy cities, killing millions of people and causing worldwide radiation poisoning. In addition, the first side to attack would probably target the enemy's communications systems. The loss of communications in warfare often leads to military defeat.

How would the United States protect its military communications in the event of a nuclear attack? Many leading scientists posed this question during the Cold War years. The problem was discussed by university professors, scientists at research institutes ("think tanks"), and officials at the Department of Defense headquarters at the Pentagon.

One researcher, Paul Baran of the RAND Corporation think tank, came up with a possible solution. The United States could create a new kind of computer communications system that did not depend on a single route to send messages. Such a system would be made up of many different points, or nodes. All of the nodes in the system would be able to send, receive, and transmit messages. Information, orders, and reports would be split into different bundles, which would be sent through the network separately and then reassembled at their destination. The system would not depend on a centralized routing system. Each node would have equal importance, and, if one or several were destroyed, other nodes would continue to function.

In 1969, the Pentagon's Advanced Research Projects Agency (ARPA) used Baran's idea to set up the ARPANET computer network. But because the Cold War had not yet turned into a real war, this

experimental system carried research data instead of military communications. High-speed computers at the University of Utah, UCLA, the Stanford Research Institute, and the University of California at Santa Barbara served as the first four nodes in the ARPANET system.

Each of ARPANET's users had an account and an address on the system, so people at different sites could share data and computer programs. For the most part, however, users sent personal messages and news on the system in a form of "electronic mail." Soon the "mailing list" system was invented, allowing a single message to be sent to "subscribers" at many different destinations. The mailing lists led to the creation of informal, long-distance clubs and

The Interface Message Processor (IMP) Development Group of ARPA, creators of ARPANET, in about 1970. Standing (left to right) are Truitt Thatch, Bill Bartell, Frank Heart, Ben Barker, Marty Thrope, Severo Ornstein, and Bob Kahn. Crouching (left to right) are Jim Geisman, Dave Walden, and Will Crowther.

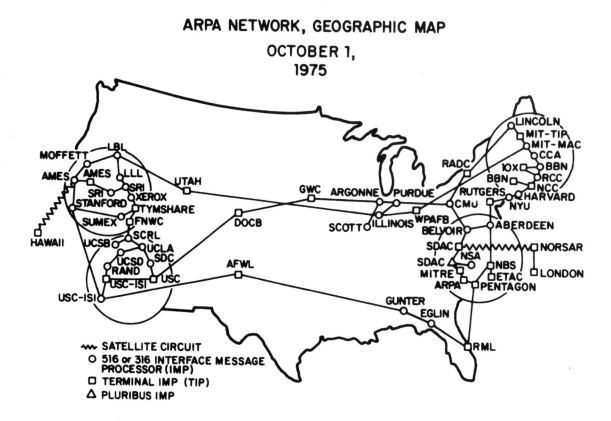

ARPA NETWORK, GEOGRAPHIC MAP
OCTOBER 1,
1975

Nodes in ARPANET as of October 1975. The first four nodes at UCLA, the University of California at Santa Barbara (UCSB), the Stanford Research Institute (SRI), and the University of Utah were joined by the RAND Corporation and five other nodes in 1971.

discussion groups devoted to such varied subjects as chess, weather forecasting, and science fiction.

In the 1980s, innovators Bob Kahn and Vint Cerf created a computer-programming language, TCP/IP, that allowed all the computers in the network to communicate with each other. TCP, or Transmission Control Protocol, converted messages into separate bundles. IP, or Internet Protocol, was the address and routing system that carried the bundles in the network to their proper destinations.

Since TCP/IP was free and available to everyone, expansion of the system beyond ARPANET's original network came rapidly. Thousands of new nodes joined the system in the 1980s, including the first overseas nodes in England and Norway.

As the network continued to grow, commercial use gradually overtook research. Telenet, the first commercial node, sold access to users in businesses and private homes. In the early 1980s, when the term "Internet" came into use, there were several hundred nodes within the system. By the end of the decade, there were more than 100,000. "E-mail," as electronic mail is now called, allowed these Internet users to send messages to any computer in the world that had an Internet address. Mailing lists and newsgroups, which work like electronic bulletin boards, linked thousands of users.

In the late 1980s, a scientist named Tim Berners-Lee began to develop a computer-programming language and system to connect information with links to make research more efficient. His language—hypertext markup language (HTML); linking system—hypertext transfer protocol (HTTP); and address system—universal resource locator (URL), became the basis of the World Wide Web, the fastest-growing segment of the Internet. With the help of "web browsers" like Marc Andreeson's widely used Netscape, the World Wide Web provides users access to almost unlimited amounts of information as well as the ability to order products marketed on the Web and comment on the text they download (bring to their computers).

Bob Kahn had been a part of ARPA's original IMP Development Group.

The Internet continues to grow without any plan or direction. Nobody screens applicants who wish to join the system, and no managers are charting the network's future. In the early 1990s, the Internet doubled in size every year. By 1996, there were nearly 50 million users worldwide. But the rapid growth of the system has brought serious problems. The high volume of Internet traffic, which is carried among the different networks over telephone lines, causes slowdowns and computer "crashes," or stoppages. Unhappy with the slowness of the Internet, some companies have begun building their own separate computer networks—known as "intranets" or "extranets"—to bypass the Internet.

In addition, an economic debate is raging over the price of using the Internet. Telephone companies believe their equipment is unfairly exploited by Internet users, most of whom pay only for inexpensive local calls and not costly long distance when they dial from their computers. These companies also fear the Internet may give its users the ability to place long-distance voice calls with their computers and thus make traditional long-distance calling by telephone obsolete.

Businesses measure the success of their websites by the number of "hits"—the number of times Internet users visit their sites.

Many people are also unhappy about the commercialization of the Internet and do not want the system used for buying and selling. As commercial Internet traffic has increased, they believe the Internet's original purpose—academic and scientific research—has suffered. A group of U.S. universities is planning Internet II, a restricted network that will carry only academic communications.

The Internet promises a future in which the once impractical utopian dream of all communications innovators—that all of the people in the world can instantly speak or write to each other—will be realized. There are many other dreams and promises attached to the system. The Internet will allow inexpensive telephone calls as well as global radio and television broadcasting. It will make the contents of all the world's libraries accessible to writers and students everywhere, and users will be able to work without leaving their homes, thus lessening traffic congestion and pollution. By communicating more readily, the world's peoples and nations might achieve a greater understanding and appreciation of each other's cultures.

There are also many possible problems in the Internet's future. As the job marketplace comes to depend on Internet knowledge, those without computers might grow poorer and less skilled. "Viruses," or destructive programs, could spread on the Internet, destroying computers and businesses, and vandals and thieves might use the Internet to break into computerized bank and credit-card accounts. The Internet even carries the risk of terrorist attacks on utilities and military installations that depend on computers.

Even if the Internet leads neither to utopia nor world destruction, there is little doubt that it will dominate the world's future communications. In fact, nearly every invention in this book—from the printed book to television—is undergoing radical changes because of this newest innovation.

Some companies have opened up radio websites where web browsers can listen to music.

The Cable News Network (CNN) and some cable companies show television clips on their websites, and companies such as First-TV are experimenting with 24-hour original television programming and film on the Internet.

A COMMUNICATIONS TIMELINE

6000 B.C.: Writing is invented in the ancient Middle East.

A.D. 700s: Woodblock printing is developed in Asia.

1040s: Movable type is invented by Pi Sheng in China.

1440s: Johann Gutenberg perfects the printing press in Germany.

1454: Gutenberg prints the 42-line "Gutenberg Bible."

late 1700s: Claude Chappé invents the semaphore system in France.

1800: In Italy, Alessandro Volta invents the battery.

1820s: Michael Faraday's electricity experiments in England promise a great future for electric power.

June 1837: Charles Wheatstone and William Cooke create an electric telegraph in England.

September 28, 1837: American Samuel Morse applies for a patent for an electric telegraph; he receives the patent in 1840.

May 24, 1844: Morse makes the first successful long-distance test of the telegraph between Baltimore, Maryland, and Washington, D.C.

1845: Morse's company builds the first commercial telegraph lines.

1851: Hiram Sibley founds the Western Union Telegraph Company.

1861: Western Union completes the first transcontinental telegraph line.

1865: James Clerk Maxwell theorizes the existence of electromagnetic waves.

July 27, 1867: The first transatlantic telegraph line is completed.

1873: The light-sensitive properties of the chemical element selenium are discovered.

March 3, 1876: Alexander Graham Bell receives a patent for his telephone on his birthday.

June 25, 1876: Bell presents his telephone invention at the Centennial Exposition in Philadelphia, Pennsylvania.

Summer 1876: Bell conducts the first telephone call over a significant distance, between Brantford and Mount Pleasant, Ontario, in Canada.

Autumn 1876: In Boston, Massachusetts, Bell conducts the first two-way telephone call.

May 1877: The first telephone system is set up in the Boston area.

December 4, 1877: Thomas Edison creates a working phonograph.

1880s: Machines that automatically cast and set type are invented.

1884: German scientist Paul Nipkow designs a mechanical-disk image scanner.

1888: Edison begins mass-producing his improved phonograph.

1888: German Heinrich Hertz generates radio waves.

March 12, 1889: American Almon B. Strowger patents an automatic telephone exchange, in which a dial is used to reach other telephones in the system.

August 13, 1889: William Gray patents the coin-operated public telephone. The telephones are introduced in Hartford, Connecticut, later that year.

1889: Edison introduces the kinetograph motion-picture camera.

November 24, 1890: In France, Edouard Branly demonstrates a radio detector, which Englishman Oliver Lodge later named a coherer.

1894: Edison introduces the kinetoscope.

1896: Guglielmo Marconi patents his wireless telegraph in England.

1899: In Denmark, Valdemar Poulsen introduces the telegraphone, ancestor of the tape recorder.

1900: German Emile Berliner brings out the disk phonograph.

December 12, 1901: Marconi receives the first transatlantic message by wireless telegraph.

early 1900s: The long-distance telephone call is made possible with signal amplifiers.

1903: Canadian Reginald Fessenden produces the liquid barretter detector that can detect voices in radio waves.

1904: J. A. Fleming creates the Fleming valve (later called the diode).

1906: Crystal detectors are discovered in the United States by H. C. Dunwoody and G. W. Pickard.

December 24, 1906: Fessenden makes the first radio broadcast off the coast of Massachusetts.

1907: Lee de Forest patents the audion.

September 22, 1912: Edwin Howard Armstrong successfully tests his regenerative circuit for a radio.

Autumn 1913: Armstrong demonstrates his regenerative-circuit radio transmitter and receiver and applies for patents for them.

March 1914: De Forest applies for a patent for his "ultra audion."

June 17, 1914: The transcontinental telephone line is completed between New York City and San Francisco.

January 25, 1915: Bell and Thomas Watson make the first transcontinental telephone call between New York City and San Francisco.

1917: Armstrong invents the superheterodyne system that allows radio receivers to tune to different frequencies.

May 19, 1922: Charles Francis Jenkins sends the first image by mechanical television in the United States.

March 1925: John Baird transmits an image with a mechanical-television system in England.

June 1925: Jenkins publicly demonstrates his mechanical-television system.

1928: Philo Farnsworth creates a working electronic-television system in the United States.

September 30, 1929: The British Broadcasting System (BBC) makes its first broadcast with mechanical television.

August 1930: Farnsworth receives a patent for his image dissector electronic-television system.

1930: Vladimir Zworykin creates the iconoscope and kinescope for RCA's electronic television.

1931: In New York City, the Columbia Broadcasting System (CBS) begins broadcasting with mechanical television.

January 24, 1933: Armstrong patents his frequency-modulation (FM) radio system.

May 21, 1934: U.S. Supreme Court rules that de Forest was the inventor of the radio.

Summer 1934: Farnsworth demonstrates his television system to the public at the Franklin Institute in Philadelphia.

1939: RCA presents television to the public at the World's Fair in New York City.

1947: AT&T scientists introduce the transistor to receive radio signals, replacing the radio tubes of Armstrong and de Forest; the first transistor radios were marketed in 1955.

1948: Long-playing records are marketed for phonographs by Columbia Records.

1954: Color television is introduced by Bell Laboratories.

1956: The first transatlantic telephone cable is completed between Great Britain, Canada, and the United States.

August 12, 1960: NASA launches the *Echo I* satellite, the first telecommunications satellite.

1960s: Cable television is introduced.

July 10, 1962: The first Telstar telecommunications satellite is launched by AT&T to improve telephone and television transmission.

November 1963: Touch-tone telephone service becomes available in Pennsylvania.

1969: The ARPANET computer network is set up by the Pentagon.

1977: The first fiber-optics communications system to improve long-distance telephone transmission and reception goes into service in Chicago, Illinois.

early 1980s: TCP/IP computer-programming language is written for the Internet system.

1980s: High-definition digital television (HDTV) is developed, but it is not introduced until the late 1990s.

1991: The World Wide Web is made possible with the computer-programming language HTML; linking system HTTP; and address system, universal resource locator.

1993: Marc Andreeson and a programming group introduce Mosaic, the first web browser.

1994: Andreeson founds a company to produce his new Netscape web browser.

2006: HDTV is predicted to completely replace electronic television.

acoustics: the study of sound and how it travels

alloy: a mixture of two or more metals

alternating current: electric current that reverses direction at regular intervals; *see also* **direct current**

amplify: to gain strength

amplitude: the greatest height or strength reached by a wave

amplitude modulation (AM): variation for radio transmission of the amplitude of a radio wave by the sound wave it carries; *see also* **frequency modulation**

anode: an electrode through which current passes from the metallic to the nonmetallic conductor; the positively charged electrode; *see also* **cathode**

antenna: an apparatus for sending and receiving electromagnetic waves

atom: the smallest unit of an element, consisting of a nucleus surrounded by electrons

audion: de Forest's radio tube, a variation of the Fleming valve vacuum tube

battery: connected cells that produce an electric current by converting chemical energy into electrical energy

broadside: a large sheet of paper printed on one side; the forerunner of the newspaper in Europe

cast: to form out of melted metal

cathode: an electrode through which current passes from the nonmetallic to the metallic conductor; the negatively charged electrode; *see also* **anode**

cathode-ray tube: a vacuum tube into which a cathode emits electrons that are in turn passed through an anode and then focused on a glowing screen; used in television sets

chase: a rectangular frame into which columns of type are locked for printing

coherer: an early detector of electrical activity

collateral: property that is used as security for a loan; if a person cannot repay a loan, the property is forfeited to the lender

compact disc: a small disc on which information or music is encoded

composing stick: a printing tool that holds the letters of a word or words to be printed

compositor: a person who sets written material into metal type; a typesetter

computer: an electronic machine that performs operations at high speed and stores and processes information

conductor: a substance that allows the transmission of electric charge

crystal detector: a piece of crystal connected to a fine metal wire that is used to detect sound waves carried by radio waves; used in early radio receivers

daguerreotype: an early type of photographic process

diaphragm: a thin disk that vibrates in response to sound waves to produce electrical signals and also vibrates in response to electrical signals to produce sound waves

direct current: electric current that flows in one direction; *see also* **alternating current**

Edison Effect: the phenomenon that a current will flow from a filament to an electrically charged plate inside a vacuum tube

electrical resistance: the opposition of a substance to current passing through it, weakening the electric current

electric circuit: a closed path followed by an electric current

electric current: the flow of electricity through a circuit

electricity: power generated by the interactions of positively and negatively charged particles (protons and electrons) in atoms

electrode: an electric conductor through which an electric current passes; cathodes and anodes are types of electrodes

electromagnet: a piece of iron wrapped in insulated wire that becomes magnetic when an electrical current runs through the wire

electromagnetic field: a field, which has both electric and magnetic components, around an electric charge in motion

electromagnetic radiation: energy in the form of traveling waves that results when an electromagnetic field produced by an electric current is disturbed because the current has been altered

electron: a particle in the atom that has a negative electrical charge

e-mail: short for electronic mail; a message sent electronically by computer to another computer in a network

facsimile: an exact copy of a document

fax machine: short for facsimile machine; a device that transmits and receives images electronically

feedback: the repeated reflowing of an electrical signal back into a circuit to increase its strength

fiber optics: the transmission of light signals through thin, flexible glass or plastic fibers; the reflection off the glass coating allows light to be transmitted even when the fiber is twisted; used in telecommunications

filament: a thinly spun wire

Fleming valve: a vacuum tube in which a small metal plate and a filament have been placed; when it is hooked up to a receiving aerial, an electrical charge flows between the filament and the metal plate inside the tube; used in early radio technology

frequency: the number of times a specific phenomenon—such as an electromagnetic wave pulse—repeats itself in one second

frequency modulation (FM): the variation for radio transmission of the frequency of a radio wave by the sound wave it carries; *see also* **amplitude modulation**

iconoscope: an early electronic-television transmitter

ideograph: a character or symbol in Asian written languages that expresses an entire word or idea, in contrast to words composed of letters

image dissector: an electronic-television transmitter that works by scanning an image line by line

induction: the generation of electric force in a circuit by varying the electromagnetic field around the circuit

interference: the prevention of clear broadcast signals

Internet: an international network of computers that allows the computers to exchange information through telephone lines

kinescope: an early electronic camera picture tube

kinetograph: a device that records a series of still images in quick succession; forerunner of the motion-picture camera

kinetoscope: a device that plays a series of still images in rapid succession; the forerunner of the movie projector

license: to grant another the right to produce and sell an invention for a fee

liquid barretter: a radio receiver developed by Reginald Fessenden

magnet: an object that attracts iron or steel and is surrounded by a magnetic field

magnetic field: an area of measurable magnetic force surrounding a magnet or electric current

matrix: a metal bar mold used in printing that is designed to receive impressions of type from which metal type can then be cast; *see also* **mold**

mechanical-disk image scanner: a device used to transmit images electronically, consisting of a large disk with holes set in a spiral pattern; light reflected off an object is passed through the holes as the disk spins and is reflected onto a selenium cell, which translates the light into electrical signals

mimeograph: a machine that makes copies of written, drawn, or typed material by means of a stencil on an inked cylinder that is pressed against sheets of paper

mint: a place where coins are manufactured

mold: in printing, the wooden piece holding the matrix from which type is cast; *see also* **matrix**

Morse code: a code of dots and dashes representing letters that Samuel Morse developed to use with the telegraph

movable type: type that can be set in a frame to print a page

node: a point on the Internet network

on-line: connected to a computer network

oscillate: to switch back and forth from alternate extremes

parchment: the skin of an animal that has been tanned and scraped thin; used for books before the use of paper became widespread in Europe

patent: to gain the exclusive right to produce and sell an invention for a period of time

photoelectric: relating to the electric properties of light, especially the movement of electrons from a substance exposed to electromagnetic waves

pitch: the highness or lowness of a sound as determined by the frequency of the sound waves

price ticker: a type of telegraph used to carry gold prices from exchange offices to the offices of gold speculators

printing press: a machine that uses movable type to print multiple copies of written materials

punch: a tool for stamping a letter or image on a surface

radio: a device used to transmit and receive electromagnetic wave signals (radio waves) that range in frequency from 10 kilohertz to 300,000 megahertz

receiver: a device that is designed to receive an electric signal and translate it into recognizable forms such as sound or print

rectification: the conversion of alternating current into direct current; detectors of radio waves rectify the waves so that sound waves can be received

regenerative circuit: an electrical circuit in which part of the circuit's output is fed back into the circuit as input, thus amplifying the signal, or making it stronger; also known as a feedback circuit

royalty: a share of the income earned on a product that is paid to an inventor in return for the right to manufacture the invention

scribe: a person who copies or writes manuscripts by hand

selenium: an element widely used in electronics because of its unusual property of being more conducive to electricity in the light than in the dark

semaphore: a method of sending messages by means of two flags—one in each hand—using an alphabetic code based on the position of the sender's arms; Claude Chappé's semaphore used mechanically controlled wooden arms

sign language: a language composed of visual signs that is used by deaf people to communicate with each other and with hearing people

spark gap: a gap in an electric circuit that electric current will jump across when given a certain electric power

telegraph: a device that, when connected to other telegraphs by wire, transmits and receives electrical signals in Morse code; duplex and multiplex telegraphs seek to send and receive more than one message simultaneously

telephone: a device that converts sound waves into electronic signals, which can be transmitted and reconverted into sound waves to permit conversation

television: a device that receives an electronic signal of an image and converts that signal into the image

Transmission Control Protocol/ Internet Protocol (TCP/IP): a computer-programming language that allows computers in a network to communicate by bundling and routing messages

transmitter: a device that generates and sends an electronic signal

type: a set of small blocks, each with a raised letter on one end, that are used for printing

Visible Speech: a set of symbols developed by Melville Bell in the nineteenth century that represented all the sounds made by the human voice; the system was used to help deaf people learn how to speak

wavelength: the distance between the peak of one wave and the peak of the next corresponding wave

wireless telegraph: a device that can send and receive electronic signals of the Morse code through the atmosphere

BIBLIOGRAPHY

Alexander, Steve. "TV's Coming to the Web." *Minneapolis Star Tribune*, March 19, 1997.

"Big Dream, Small Screen." *The American Experience*. Boston: WGBH, 1997. television program.

Buranelli, Vincent. *Thomas Alva Edison*. Englewood Cliffs, N.J.: Silver Burdett, 1989.

Burch, Joann Johansen. *Fine Print: A Story about Johann Gutenberg*. Minneapolis: Carolrhoda, 1991.

Chappell, Warren. *A Short History of the Printed Word*. New York: Knopf, 1970.

Coe, Douglas. *Marconi: Pioneer of Radio*. New York: Julian Messner, 1943.

Coe, Lewis. *The Telegraph: A History of Morse's Invention and its Predecessors in the United States*. Jefferson, N.C.: McFarland, 1993.

Conot, Robert. *Thomas A. Edison: A Streak of Luck*. New York: Da Capo Press, 1979.

"The Economics of the Internet." *The Economist*, October 19, 1996.

Everson, George. *The Story of Television: The Life of Philo T. Farnsworth*. New York: W. W. Norton, 1949.

Farnsworth, Elma G. *Distant Vision: Romance and Discovery of an Invisible Frontier*. Salt Lake City: PemberlyKent, 1989.

Febvre, Lucien, and Henri-Jean Martin. *The Coming of the Book: The Impact of Printing, 1450-1800*. trans. David Gerard. London: Verso, 1984.

Giscard d'Estaing, Valérie-Anne. *The Second World Almanac Book of Inventions*. New York: World Almanac, 1986.

Greene, Carol. *Thomas Alva Edison: Bringer of Light*. Chicago: Childrens Press, 1985.

Harris, Brayton. *Johann Gutenberg and the Invention of Printing*. New York: Franklin Watts, 1972.

Hays, Wilma. *Samuel Morse and the Electronic Age*. New York: Franklin Watts, 1966.

"History of Television, Part 1." Pavek Museum Newsletter, Summer 1991.

House, G. W. O. "Edwin H. Armstrong." *Wireless Engineer*, March 1954.

Jolly, W. P. *Marconi*. New York: Stein and Day, 1972.

Josephson, Matthew. *Edison: A Biography*. New York: J. Wiley and Sons, 1992.

Kane, Joseph Nathan. *Famous First Facts*. 4th ed. New York: H. W. Wilson, 1981.

Kerby, Mona. *Samuel Morse*. New York: Franklin Watts, 1991.

Krensky, Stephen. *Breaking into Print: Before and After the Invention of the Printing Press*. Boston: Little, Brown, 1996.

Lampton, Christopher. *Thomas Alva Edison*. New York: Franklin Watts, 1988.

Lessing, Lawrence P. *Man of High Fidelity*. Philadelphia: Lippincott, 1956.

Lewis, Cynthia Copeland. *Hello, Alexander Graham Bell Speaking: A Biography*. Minneapolis: Dillon Press, 1991.

Lewis, Tom. *Empire of the Air: The Men Who Made Radio*. New York: HarperCollins, 1991.

"The Man Who Invented the Web." *Time*, May 19, 1997.

Marconi, Degna. *My Father, Marconi*. New York: McGraw-Hill, 1962.

Mitchell, Barbara. *The Wizard of Sound: A Story about Thomas Edison*. Minneapolis: Carolrhoda, 1991.

Mitchell, Curtiss. *Cavalcade of Broadcasting*. Chicago: Follett, 1970.

Pelta, Kathy. *Alexander Graham Bell*. Englewood Cliffs, N.J.: Silver Burdett, 1989.

Quiri, Patricia Ryon. *Alexander Graham Bell*. New York: Franklin Watts, 1991.

Raymer, S. N. "Fessenden Revisited." unpublished article.

Sterling, Bruce. "Internet." *The Magazine of Fantasy and Science Fiction*, February 1993.

"The Telephone." *The American Experience*. Boston: WGBH, 1997. television program.

"A Tube for Tomorrow." *Time*, April 14, 1997.

Udelson, Joseph H. *The Great Television Race*. Tuscaloosa: University of Alabama Press, 1982.

Weise, Elizabeth. "Gates, McCaw Hope to Take Internet Worldwide." *Minneapolis Star Tribune*, March 17, 1997.

INDEX

ABOUT THE AUTHOR

Thomas Streissguth is the author of numerous books for young people, including The Oliver Press titles *Hatemongers and Demagogues, Soviet Leaders from Lenin to Gorbachev, International Terrorists, Hoaxers and Hustlers, Charismatic Cult Leaders, Legendary Labor Leaders*, and *Utopian Visionaries*. A graduate of Yale University, Streissguth has worked as a teacher, editor, and journalist, as well as a writer. After living for a year in the French countryside, Streissguth and his wife and two daughters now make their home in Sarasota, Florida.

PHOTO ACKNOWLEDGMENTS

Archive Photos: pp. 54, 55, 75, 84 (top), 98, 113, 118
Archive Photos/ American Stock: pp. 51, 72
Archive Photos/ AMW Pressedienst GMBH: p. 120
Archive Photos/ *Illustrated London News*: p. 85
The Bettmann Archive: pp. 40, 89
Brigham Young University Archives: p. 119
Charles Babbage Institute, University of Minnesota: pp. 123, 124
Corbis/ Bettmann: p. 80
Harry S. Truman Library: p. 122 (top)
Library of Congress: pp. 6, 7, 8, 9, 12, 14, 15, 16, 18, 20, 21, 23, 26, 30, 31, 33, 34, 36, 38 (both), 39, 45, 47, 48 (both), 49, 52 (both), 53, 63, 70, 71, 83, 86, 97, 105, 106

Marylandia Collection, University of Maryland: pp. 2, 102, 110, 116
National Library of Medicine: p. 10
Pavek Museum of Broadcasting: pp. 92, 100
RAND Corporation: p. 122 (bottom)
Rick Wacha: pp. 76, 82, 84 (bottom), 88, 90, 91, 93, 101, 114
UPI/ Bettmann: p. 115
U.S. Department of the Interior, National Park Service, Edison National Historic Site: pp. 44, 56, 58, 61, 64, 65, 66, 67, 69

The publisher wishes to thank the Pavek Museum of Broadcasting in St. Louis Park, Minnesota, for graciously allowing items in its collection to be photographed for this book.